DEADLY REDEMPTION

RICHARD REES

Copyright © Richard Rees 2009

First printed in this edition 2020

www.richardhrees.com

The right of Richard Rees to be identified as the author of this work has been asserted by him in accordance with the Copyright, Designs and Patents Act, 1988

This book is sold subject to the condition that it shall not, by way of trade or otherwise, be lent, resold, hired out, or otherwise circulated without the author's prior consent in any form of binding or cover other than that in which it is published and without a similar condition being imposed on the subsequent purchaser.

ISBN: 979-8-6651394-9-4

Front cover design by author: Richard Rees

Book design: Dean Fetzer, www.gunboss.com

To Dean Fetzer, for all his help and expertise in placing my novels and screenplays on Amazon Direct Publishing, and on Kindle, which I don't have a clue how to do. Our association over the years is now a friendship, and though we've never met, I hope one day we will.

Foreword

The thought that led to the premise for DEADLY REDEMPTION originated from watching the film *Sliding Doors*. The WHAT IF? factor. The movie is in effect two stories. One tells how the life of its female lead would have resulted if she'd caught a London Underground train after finishing work earlier than usual, only for its sliding doors to close on her just as she's about to enter it. The other asks "what if" she was a *second* sooner and caught the train? And got home before her normal time, only to find her boyfriend in bed with another woman? How would her future life then have been?

The WHAT IF factor also affects *our* lives. What if one's mother and father hadn't met? First, we wouldn't have been born. And therefore, inherited our particular genes. Or experienced the environmental elements that surround us, or had the education, good or bad, that affects our lives, wealthy or poor. Most of the factors that had a bearing on my life, past and present, are given in my book, *Dear Abigail*, and influenced my decision to give up accountancy to try to become a writer. One of my previously published novels, *Somebody Wants To Kill Me*, was first written as a screenplay, then changed to a novel. But with *Deadly Redemption,* I thought it was best told filmicly, and although its plot-line is given in the following synopsis, I hope it's enjoyed by those of you who opt to read it in script format.

I set the story in New York rather than London. Though both are monied cities, with wealthy people to whom the male protagonist's fee (though it would be big to him) would be petty cash to them to achieve their aim, it's also a "melting pot" (a metaphor first coined in 1908) to describe its union of many nationalities, cultures, ethnicities, languages (over 800). It also has Greenwich Village where my male protagonist lives, a Japanese Garden, and a Japanese cemetery, which is important to him. Furthermore, I needed a rocky shoreline close to the city (which London doesn't have) for a crucial scene. And where better than Long Island's North Shore, overlooking its wide and deep Sound?

Having decided this, I was back to WHAT IF? Though my protagonist turns into a serial killer, I needed him to have a reason for choosing the path he takes. So, WHAT IF he's the product of a mixed marriage, influenced not only by his white American mother, but mostly his Japanese father, and beliefs that go back centuries? This inborn conflict within him is shown in a simple flashback scene of him as a child walking through a park holding their hands. They come to a fork in the path. His mother wants to go right. His father left, to the Japanese Garden section and its Shinto shrine. His mother gives in. They go left. And so, at the point in my story where he has to choose *his* path, he follows his father's psyche. But then, to add drama to the story, WHAT IF it also has a female protagonist determined to find the man she believes caused her sister's suicide, and is seeking revenge for it. And so begins her hunt to track him down. And his determination to stay one step ahead of her, and achieve redemption for his past sins.

His DEADLY REDEMPTION.

But for which one of them? Him? Or her?

Richard Rees
www.richardhrees.com

Deadly Redemption

A screenplay

Historical Drama/Love Story

Length: 102 pages

Logline

Once he killed marriages for a living. Now he lives to kill those who paid him.

Synopsis

JOHN NAKATA, half Caucasian American, half Japanese, is a Wakaresaseya, "a breaker-up" of marriages. His modus operandi, for which he charges a big fee, is to seduce wives of husbands who require filmed evidence of it to discard them for younger and more glamorous women.

A tragedy in Nakata's own life hardened his heart. Losing his adored wife to illness, he wanted the best for his 2-year-old daughter, Emma, and left her in his sister Liz's care while he moved to New York to make big bucks for him to return wealthy to Emma.

But then the Japanese Shinto side of his nature broods about the harm he's doing. Can he first achieve redemption for all the evil he has committed, before going back to Emma? He decides his path is to ritually kill ten of the husbands who paid him to seduce their wives and so avenge them. And to make their deaths seem like suicides, so leaving no trail for him to be discovered as their killer. Convinced that this would be the Shinto way, he begins his quest.

But also back home in New York, is LISA PERANO, a hardened ex-marine who's there to find the answer as to why her unhappily married sister took her own life only days after meeting a man who she seemingly fell madly in love with on first sight and let herself to be seduced by him the same night. Lisa can't understand the contradiction of it and vows to find the man.

Enlisting the help of her best friend, GINA CAMBI, a newspaper crime reporter, they're led to a string of seemingly motiveless suicides of wealthy men, but with a common pattern. All have divorced their wives for adultery and replaced them with younger women. Even more, the description of the man who seduced their wives, fits the stranger who seduced Anna.

Convinced it's the same man, Lisa sets out to track him down and avenge Anna.

He's a killer. She's an ex-marine trained to kill.

What will happen when they meet?

DEADLY REDEMPTION

Richard Rees

WGAw

FADE IN

INT. HOTEL SUITE #1, NEW YORK - DAY

Sounds of a man and a woman making love come from bedroom. She climaxes, soft moans, is briefly silent, exhales, sated.

                    GRACE PERRY (O.S.)
          Now *that* was something else. I
          only wish I could stay longer
          and do it over and over again.
              (reluctant)
          But I'd best be getting back or
          he'll be asking questions.

INT. BEDROOM, HOTEL SUITE #1 - DAY

JOHN NAKATA, 35, half Caucasian American, half Japanese, sits up in bed, half covered by duvet. He's tall, dark, handsome.

GRACE PERRY, 40, gets out of bed, gathers-up her scattered clothes, checks watch.

                    GRACE PERRY (CONT'D)
          Hell, just look at the time! I'll
          shower when I get home.
              (enters bathroom)

Nakata watches her reflected in a long bedroom mirror as she hurriedly dresses, repairs make-up, hair, re-enters bedroom.

                    GRACE PERRY (CONT'D)
          Maybe we can meet again?

                    NAKATA
          Give me your number.

Hands her a BLACK cell-phone. She enters number. Hurriedly kisses him, regrets having to leave. Pauses at bedroom door.

                    GRACE PERRY
          Until next time.

EXITS to sitting room, and from suite.

Nakata gets out of bed, checks hidden camera that lovemaking has been filmed, Grace Perry facing the lens, his back to it.

Gets dressed. Bags camera. EXITS suite.

INT. A ROMAN CATHOLIC CHURCH, GREENWICH - DAY

LISA PERANO, 30, blonde, pretty, wearing black, kneels in a pew, praying to a Cross of Christ Crucified hanging on wall.

FATHER O'DONNELL, an elderly priest who's known Lisa since birth enters from Vestry, sits in pew in front of her.

                    LISA
          Father.

                    O'DONNELL
                (compassionate)
          I was sorry to hear about Nick, Lisa.
          How long is your furlough?

                    LISA
          For good, Father. But in one piece.
                (bitter)
          Unlike Nick. Road bomb. There weren't
          enough bits of him left to bring home
          in a body bag.

                    O'DONNELL
          I will pray for his soul, Lisa.

                    LISA
          Don't bother, Father. He gave God up.
          Afghanistan or Hell. Christian or
          Islam. It came to the point he said
          he couldn't tell the difference.

                    O'DONNELL
          The danger came with the territory,
          Lisa, not God. You were soldiers -

                    LISA
          Chaplain blessed us. Next day, Nick
          was dead.

                    O'DONNELL
          The Lord's ways are not our ways,
          Lisa. It is not given to us to
          understand His purposes -

                    LISA
          I'm nor here for Nick, Father. Or
          for myself. I think the same as he
          did. I'm here for Anna. Why did she
          do what she did? Do *you* know?

                    O'DONNELL
          I'm sorry, Lisa, I don't. I know
          she was unhappy in her marriage. She
          came to me to discuss it, not in the
          confessional, so I'm able to –

                    LISA
          I know all about that, Father. She
          should never have married the lech.
          I warned her about him. But ...

Lisa produces an airmail letter but doesn't open it.

                    LISA (CONT'D)
          ... this was her last letter to me.
          She'd just met someone else. Typical
          of Anna; she fell for him on their
          very first date. Heart. And body -
          Sorry, Father. She was over the moon.

                    O'DONNELL
                    (mildly chastening)
          Lisa. You know the Church can never
          condone infidelity, whatever the -

                    LISA
                    (snappy)
          I know that, Father. The point I'm
          making is that she was suddenly happy
          again. Yet, next thing I hear, she's
          taken her life.

Stuffs airmail back in pocket, gets to her feet.

                    LISA (CONT'D)
          Well, I'm not going to rest until
          I find out why.

Heads up aisle. O'Donnell makes sign of the Cross.

INT. NAKATA'S APARTMENT, EAST VILLAGE - DAY

Large apartment is the first floor of a brownstone house.

Décor is mix of modern Western and ancient-style Japanese furniture, paintings, pottery. All fine taste, expensive.

On wall above a side-table, is a Japanese-style painting of Nakata and late wife, RACHEL, 30, Caucasian American, both in black sashed robes; with blossom tree, Japanese sunset.

Nakata ENTERS, puts film camera on an antique desk, pours a whiskey, tosses it down like he really needs it.

Connects camera to laptop, copies film of Grace Perry and himself making love to a DVD. Then a STILL PHOTO from it to his black cell - Grace's face visible, his hidden.

Extracts black, leather-bound LEDGER from drawer, opens it to last recorded double page. It shows facial photo of Grace. And DAVID PERRY, 45. Cell number. PO BOX number.

Ledger's earlier pages, to start of book, record details and photos of other previous "clients" and wives.

Nakata calls - on his black cell - Perry's cell-phone.

INT. PERRY'S LUXURY APARTMENT - DAY

Perry waits in his study, door closed, for Nakata to call. His cell rings. Snatches it on, answers, voice low.

PERRY
Perry.

NAKATA (O.S.)
I've got your evidence. I'll send it when I get my fee.

PERRY
I need proof first.

INT. NAKATA'S APARTMENT - DAY

Nakata sends Perry the still photo of Grace and himself.

PERRY (O.S. CONT'D)
The bitch. Was she easy?

NAKATA
You wanted evidence, not details.

PERRY (O.S. CONT'D)
One picture's not enough. I need the film of it.

NAKATA
When your fee's in my account.

Nakata ends the call, enters his online bank account. Pours another whiskey and waits, sipping it. $25,000 pings in.

Writes PAID across Perry's page, replaces Ledger in drawer, puts DVD in a USPS bag, addresses it to the Box number.

Picks up whiskey bottle and, from mantelshelf a framed photo of daughter EMMA, then 2, with Rachel. Takes them to a sofa.

Lies on sofa, lovingly touches Emma's and Rachel's faces.

INT. LISA'S APARTMENT, QUEENS - DAY

Apartment is small. Lisa ENTERS, still wearing black, sits, produces Anna's letter, reads it, hearing Anna's voice.

ANNA (V.O.)
He's fantastic, Lise. Perfect manners, not brash. Treated me like a lady. The opposite of Tony. Okay, so we fell into bed on our first meeting. But what the hell, life's for living.

Lisa closes her eyes, thinking of Anna, returns to letter.

>   ANNA (V.O. CONT'D)
>   What's more, he's tall, dark, and
>   handsome, as they say. And as for
>   his lovemaking, then WOW!

Lisa can't take any more, flings letter aside. Picks up a phone-book from coffee table, finds a number, calls it.

GINA CAMBI, 30, answers.

>   GINA (O.S)
>   Gina Cambi. Newsroom.

>   LISA
>   Gina, it's Lisa.

>   GINA (O.S.)
>   Lise. I heard you were home. I'm
>   so sorry about Anna. She was a
>   great kid.

>   LISA
>   The best.

INT. BUSY NEWSROOM, NEWSPAPER OFFICE - NIGHT

Gina, a newspaper reporter, sits at a cluttered desk. She's as dark haired as Lisa is blonde, and also pretty.

>   GINA
>   Sorry to hear about Nick, too.

>   LISA (O.S.)
>   Thanks, Gina.

>   GINA
>   Any time you'd like to call. I
>   still live in the same apartment.

>   LISA (O.S.)
>   It's what I was hoping, Gina. When?

>   GINA
>   Let me check my diary.
>   (does so)
>   How about ...

INT. LISA'S APARTMENT - NIGHT

>   LISA
>   (notes day and time)
>   Fine, Gina. See you then.

Lisa ends call. Picks up photo on coffee table of ANNA, 28, pretty, fair haired like herself. Sheds tear for her sister.

INT. NAKATA'S APARTMENT - DAY

Nakata still holds photo of Rachel and Emma, swigs from the whiskey bottle, trying to dull his inner pain.

Nakata turns photo face down, hurts him to see them. Takes another slug of whiskey, wants oblivion.

LATER

Nakata sleeps on sofa. He's found oblivion.

EXT. MONDE ART GALLERY, CHELSEA - DAY

The gallery sells Western and Japanese art. Nakata approaches wearing dark-blue casual clothes, dark sun glasses. ENTERS.

Seen through window, he crosses to MONDE, 50, medium height, dapper. They discuss a yellow canvas, prominently displayed.

INT. MONDE ART GALLERY - DAY

The painting is a Lucio Fontana, entitled: Concetto Spaziale, Attese, 1966. It has three downward slashes: two V-shaped but apart and one between them - vaginal-like.

Monde extols the painting to Nakata, layers it on.

      MONDE
  The fascination of a Fontana for me,
  is the mystical, yet sensual quality
  of his work. Symbolizing not only the
  female form but also its penetration,
  emphasizing the mental in terms of
  the physical -

      NAKATA
  To me, a Fontana always says: Anger.
  Rage.

      MONDE
    (taken aback)
  Do they, indeed?

      NAKATA
  At the seeming cruelty of life. Each
  cut screaming why?

      MONDE
  Ah, well. To the eye of the beholder.

                    NAKATA
          How much?

                    MONDE
          More than you usually pay, I regret.
          Eight hundred thousand ...?
                (sees Nakata hesitate)
          At Sotheby's or Christie's it would
          fetch considerably more.

Nakata regretfully shakes his head. But Monde is not one
to let a buyer go. Looks around, ensures they're alone.

                    MONDE (CONT'D)
          I may be able find someone to paint
          you one ... very similar?

Nakata realises Monde means a fake. Nods.

                    MONDE (CONT'D)
          If you'd come through to my office.

INT. OFFICE, MONDE ART GALLERY - DAY

Seen through an inner window, Monde is back in the gallery,
having left Nakata alone to talk to the forger.

Nakata sits at a laptop, a phone to his ear as he searches a
website with illustrations of Fontana's works. Pauses at one
resembling a Buddha-like stomach, copper-coloured, seemingly
holed by a blunt-pointed instrument. Says to forger on phone.

                    NAKATA
          What about his Concetto spaziale,
          1962? Owned by the Carnegie Museum?

INT. SLOVAK'S STUDIO, BOWERY - DAY

JAN SLOVAK, 40, checks the illustration on a computer screen.
The studio/living room is on second floor of an ex-warehouse.

                    SLOVAK
          It's in copper. As in metal. I do
          only canvases.

INT. OFFICE, MONDE ART GALLERY - DAY

Nakata scrolls more illustrations, pauses at one of a blood
red canvas, V-slashed, but apart. Again questions forger.

                    NAKATA
          Concetto Spaciale, attese, 1960?
          Museum of Fine Arts, Houston.

INT. SLOVAK'S STUDIO - DAY

Slovak studies same illustration.

                    SLOVAK
Yeah. That I can do. Twenty K.

                    NAKATA (O.S.)
Ten.

                    SLOVAK
Fifteen.

                    NAKATA (O.S)
Ten. Cash.

                    SLOVAK
You bargain fucking hard, friend.
Pick it up day after tomorrow.

                    NAKATA (O.S.)
Address?

INT. OFFICE, MONDE ART GALLERY - DAY

Nakata notes Novak's address, pockets it, exits office.

Seen through inner window to gallery, Monde questions him. Nakata curtly replies, EXITS gallery.

INT. MONDE ART GALLERY - DAY

Monde watches Nakata go, redials from gallery extension.

INT. SLOVAK'S STUDIO - DAY

Slovak answers his phone.

                    SLOVAK
Slovak.

                    MONDE (O.S.)
How much?

                    SLOVAK
Ten.

                    MONDE (O.S.)
You could have got twenty. I should
double my percentage on it.

                    SLOVAK
You wish. That it?

                    MONDE (O.S.)
          When he comes to collect it, get his
          vehicle license details.

                    SLOVAK
          What for?

INT. MONDE ART GALLERY - DAY

Monde affects but curiosity in Nakata.

                    MONDE
          Just interested. Always pays cash.

                    SLOVAK (O.S)
          Best kinda buyer to have. But no can
          do. I'm an artist not a snoop.
               (ends call)

Monde returns to the window. There's no sign of Nakata.

INT. NAKATA'S APARTMENT - DAY

Nakata enters. Black cell rings. Answers it.

                    NAKATA
          Karesa Agency.

INT. WARNER'S LUXURY APARTMENT - DAY

BOB WARNER, 40, replies on cell-phone, from sitting room.
He's self-assertive, bumptious.

                    WARNER
          A friend's given me your number.
          You did him a service.

SUSAN WARNER, 35, fair hair, pretty, unaffected, ENTERS.

                    WARNER (CONT'D)
               (curt)
          I'm talking to a client.

                    SUSAN
          Sorry.

She EXITS. Warner lowers his voice to Nakata.

                    WARNER (CONT'D)
          As I was saying you did him a -

                    NAKATA (O.S.)
          Sam's Tavern on Irving. One hour.

INT. NAKATA'S APARTMENT - DAY

Warner, still on his cell, describes himself to Nakata.

                    WARNER (O.S.)
          I'm five ten, brownish hair -

Nakata cuts across him.

                    NAKATA
          I'll recognize you.

Ends call, adds to himself

                    NAKATA (CONT'D)
          You all have that same shifty look
          in your eyes.

Nakata phones out. O'NEILL, 45, backstreet P.I., answers.

                    O'NEILL (O.S.)
          O'Neill.

                    NAKATA
          Karesa. Sam's Tavern. One hour.

                    O'NEILL (O.S. CONT'D)
          I'll be there.

EXT. SAM'S TAVERN, EAST VILLAGE - DAY

Nakata approaches, enters tavern.

Viewed through a window, he spots Warner at a table, sits opposite him. Warner offers his hand. Nakata ignores it.

INT. SAM'S TAVERN - DAY

Nakata produces notebook. Warner questions him first.

                    WARNER
          Your fee?

                    NAKATA
              (curt)
          Twenty-five grand.

                    WARNER
          Worth every cent. Variety's the
          spice of life - so it's said. I
          get bored with the same old -

                    NAKATA
          I don't get personally involved.

EXT. SAM'S TAVERN - DAY

Viewed through window. Nakata questions Warner, enters the replies in note book, asks for a PHOTO, pockets it. EXITS.

Nakata nods to O'Neill, hiding in cover. Heads down Irving.

Warner exits. Heads up Irving. O'Neill follows.

A waiting BIMBO takes Warner's arm, questions him as they walk, laughing at their success with Nakata.

INT. NAKATA'S APARTMENT - DAY

Nakata copies photo of Susan Warner to black cell.

Cell pings. O'Neill sends him photo of Warner, and data: address, landline phone number.

Nakata enters date in next blank, double-page of Ledger, and from his note book, Warner's cell number.

Nakata connects his cell to a printer, prints Warner's and Susan's photos, pastes them below data, adds PO box number.

Dials Warner's cell number. Warner answers.

                    NAKATA
Karesa. Your PO box number is ...

INT. AN OPERA HOUSE - NIGHT

Susan Warner sits alone. The seat next to hers is empty.

Nakata walks down aisle, checks ticket, sits next to her. She studies him from corner of eye. He says aside to her.

                    NAKATA
I was lucky to get this seat. A late cancellation.

                    SUSAN
            (hesitant, shy)
It was my husband's. His usual excuse. Business. Much more important.

                    NAKATA
Then he has his priorities wrong.
            (offers his hand)
Thomas Oshiro.

                    SUSAN
            (shyly shakes hand)
Susan Warner.

The opera, *Don Giovanni*, starts. Susan, on the pretence of moving her head to see better, moves closer to Nakata.

INT. OPERA HOUSE - NIGHT

On stage, setting is a piazza outside Don Giovanni's palace. Don Giovanni, wearing black, holds a fair-haired bride, in a white wedding gown, in his arms.

Nakata glances at Susan's fair hair.

              NAKATA
    That could be you up there, being
    seduced by Don Giovanni.

              SUSAN
    Oh, I hardly think so.

              NAKATA
    On the contrary, I think he'd find
    you irresistible.

A Woman behind them "SUSHES" them. Nakata, Susan, exchange amused glances, return their attention to *Don Giovanni*.

Susan smiles to herself at Nakata's compliment.

LATER

Curtain falls on Act One. Susan's very aware of Nakata.

              NAKATA
    Don Giovanni both fascinates and
    disturbs me.

              SUSAN
    Il dissolute punito, to give it it's
    full title. The Rake Punished.

              NAKATA
    He deserves to be. Some six hundred
    seductions in Italy. Two hundred in
    Germany. A thousand in Spain.

              SUSAN
    Still, he must have had something
    about him. Add the ones in France
    and Turkey, over two thousand women
    fell for his charm.

Silence. She's even more aware of Nakata. He undertones.

              NAKATA
    Coffee? Before Act Two? My hotel
    is just around the corner?

Susan suspects Nakata's meaning, hesitates, finds courage.

                    SUSAN
Yes. That would be very nice.

                    NAKATA
The hotel lounge? Or my suite?.

                    SUSAN
        (takes plunge)
Your suite.

INT. GINA CAMBI'S MODEST APARTMENT - NIGHT

Gina and Lisa sit, sipping wine. Gina studies Nick's photo, wearing army combats.

                    GINA
He looks nice. Good looking, too.
        (returns photo to Lisa)

                    LISA
He was. Both.
        (pauses)
What can you tell me about Anna's man friend? How long had she known him before she went out with him?

                    GINA
        (hesitates to reply)
I'm sorry, Lisa. As far as I know, she met him only once -

                    LISA
Once! You telling me Anna killed herself over a one-night stand!

                    GINA
She called me next morning, to tell me about him. She'd fallen for him, big-time. Next I hear, she'd taken an overdose.

                    LISA
So, you know *nothing* about him?

                    GINA
Sorry.

Lisa broods, suddenly decides.

                    LISA
Then I guess I've no choice but to start with Tony - Even though he's the slimeball who drove her to it.

Gina clasps Lisa's hand - telling she's in this, too.

                    GINA
          WE'LL have to start. Between us
          we'll find out why she did it.
          The new Cagney and Lacey.

Clasping hands, they intone, tad wistful, opening bars to "Cagney and Lacey" theme tune, determined to solve "why".

INT. BEDROOM, HOTEL SUITE #2 - NIGHT

Nakata sits in bed, zips-up Susan's dress. She's loath to go.

                    SUSAN
          I don't want to go. But if I'm not
          home soon, he'll create holy hell.
                    (hesitates to ask)
          Do you think we might ... ?

Nakata produces his black cell.

                    NAKATA
          Give me your cell number?

Susan, bolder now, takes cell, enters it, returns cell.

                    SUSAN
          You *will* call me?

                    NAKATA
          Tomorrow, without fail.

She still needs reassurance.

                    SUSAN
          Mid-morning? He's usually out at
          that time.

Nakata kisses his finger-tips, puts them to Susan's lips. She kisses them, happy, believing him. EXITS the suite.

Nakata screws his eyes closed, hating this seduction.

INT. NAKATA'S APARTMENT - NIGHT

Nakata's at his desk, bank account online, Ledger open at Warner's page, DVD ready to post, ringing cell to his ear.

He drinks large whiskey, trying to blot out his guilt over Susan - he liked her. He's curt when Warner answers call.

                    NAKATA
          I've got your *evidence*.

Warner questions back.

                    NAKATA (CONT'D)
               (snaps back)
          When I get my fee.

Warner queries. Hardly able to look at it, Nakata sends him photo of Susan and he making love. Warner still questions.

                    NAKATA (CONT'D)
          Twenty five. As agreed.

Nakata almost snarls at Warner's response.

                    NAKATA (CONT'D)
          High? Compared to the pittance of
          a settlement you'll force on her?

Warner still argues.

                    NAKATA (CONT'D)
               (really snaps)
          Five minutes or I'll destroy it.

Cuts call, gulps rest of whiskey while waiting.

$25K enters Nakata's bank account. Scrawls *PAID* on Warner's page, savagely slides Ledger into a drawer, slams it shut.

Swipes an ornate Japanese paperweight off desk. It shatters.

Moves to sofa. Looks at Emma's and Rachel's photo. Broods.

FLASHBACK:

EXT. JAPANESE SECTION, MOUNT OLIVET CEMETERY, QUEENS - DAY

Nakata and his sister MEG, 30, stand by open grave, holding 2-year old EMMA's hands, looking down at coffin's name plate.

RACHEL NAKATA
   AGED 30

Nakata, heart-broken, scatters earth on coffin. Emma raises up her arms to him.

                    EMMA
          Daddy.

Nakata lifts her up. She wraps her arms around his neck. He walks away with Meg holding his arm.

INT. NAKATA'S APARTMENT - NIGHT

Nakata still broods on the sofa. Gets another FLASHBACK.

FLASHBACK

INT. NAKATA'S PREVIOUS HOUSE - DAY

Sitting room, modestly furnished.

It's shortly after Rachel's funeral. Nakata's packed bags are in Hall. Emma, listens, bemused, as Meg begs with him.

                    MEG
      Please don't go, John. Emma needs you.

                    NAKATA
      I have to, Meg. She's always going to
      have the best. And I can't provide her
      with that around here.

Emma runs to him, wraps her arms around his legs. Nakata holds her tight, loath to leave her. Explains more to Meg.

                    NAKATA (CONT'D)
      It's just for a couple of years. Until
      I've made enough for us to start a new
      life.

                    MEG
      She needs your love, John. Not money.

                    NAKATA
      This way I'll be giving her both.

                    MEG
      But what are you going to do when you
      get to New York?

                    NAKATA
      I don't know. I'll find something.

Abruptly gives Emma to Meg, picks up his bags. EXITS.

INT. NAKATA'S APARTMENT - NIGHT

Still lying on the sofa, Nakata IMAGINES Rachel sitting next to him, reproaching him.

                    RACHEL
      You were wrong, John.

                    NAKATA
      If I could turn the clock back, Rach,
      I would. But I can't. Not with what
      I've become.

                    RACHEL
      Oh, John.

                    NAKATA
          I needed to give Emma the very best.
          Though I hate myself for it, it's the
          only way I could find to make enough
          to return to her as soon as I might.

Rachel extends hand to him. He reaches for it. She fades away. Tears well in Nakata's eyes. He exits on to his:

BALCONY, looks over the rail.

Quiet, leafy street below seems to pull him down toward it. He's transfixed, feels like he's falling, falling ...

SHRILL, SHRILL ... SHRILL, SHRILL.

Ringing of Nakata's LANDLINE jerks him back. Enters sitting room, sees MEG on phone screen. Answers it.

                    NAKATA
          Meg! It's so good to hear you.

                    MEG (O.S)
          You could hear me more often – and
          I you – if you sometimes called. I
          don't even have a photo of you and
          getting to forget what you look like.
          It's been so long since I saw you.

                    NAKATA
          Meg, I'm sorry, but I've been -

                    MEG (O.S.)
          I know. Busy as ever. But I didn't
          call to scold you, John.

INT. MEG'S NEW HOUSE - NIGHT

Big sitting room. Packing crates show Meg's just moved in.

Meg's starting to show she's pregnant. Emma, now 5, is with her. Emma yawns, tired, it's been a long day.

                    MEG
          I just wanted to tell you the house
          is ... Oh, John, it's the home of my
          dreams. And to say thank you for it.
          It's ... it's the best. As are you.

Takes Emma's hand.

                    MEG (CONT'D)
          Emma and I are going to be so happy
          here. Even happier when you come and
          see it for yourself.

Meg touches her womb.

                    MEG (CONT'D)
          When I may have a little surprise
          for you.

Emma tugs Meg's skirt.

                    MEG (CONT'D)
          But I've a very tired little girl
          here who very much wants to talk to
          her Daddy before she goes to bed.

Gives Emma the phone.

                    EMMA
          Daddy!

INT. NAKATA'S APARTMENT - NIGHT

Nakata's tears well again as he hears Emma's voice.

                    NAKATA
          Hello, angel. I've missed you.

Hears Emma say to Meg.

                    EMMA (O.S.)
          It's not Daddy.

                    MEG (O.S.)
          Of course it is, Emma.

INT. MEG'S HOUSE - NIGHT

Emma, pouting, gives phone back to Meg.

                    EMMA
          No it's not!

Runs to a chair, hugs a Teddy. Meg explains to Nakata.

                    MEG
          I'm sorry John, it's just that she's
          tired, and hasn't seen or spoken to
          you for such a long time now.

INT. NAKATA'S APARTMENT - NIGHT

                    NAKATA
          It's okay, Meg, I understand. I'll
          come and see you both soon ... Once
          you've settled in.

                    MEG (O.S.)
              Promise?

Nakata fills with emotion as he lies to Meg.

                    NAKATA
              I promise.
                   (chokes)
              I have to go, there's someone on my
              other line.

Cuts call, drops onto sofa, stretches out on it.

Again IMAGINES Rachel sitting by him; eyes reproach him.

                    NAKATA (CONT'D)
              Except I can't, Rach, I can't. Not
              with what I've become. I'm beyond
              redemption.

Rachel fades away. Nakata stares after her, a man lost.

INT. LISA'S APARTMENT - NIGHT

Lisa checks a number in her phone diary, calls it.
TONY FALCO, 35, Anna's ex-husband, answers.

                    FALCO (O.S)
              Tony Falco.

Lisa replies, curt, she's never liked Tony.

                    LISA
              It's Lisa. I'd like to come over
              and talk to you about Anna.

INT. FALCO'S LUXURY APARTMENT, QUEENS - NIGHT

Falco's handsome, but a heel. And smug with it.

                    FALCO
              And I don't want to talk to *you*.

                    LISA (O.S)
              Tony -

                    FALCO
              Fuck off.
                   (cuts call)

INT. LISA'S APARTMENT - NIGHT

Lisa phones Gina at her news-desk.

Gina answers to background sounds of a busy newsroom.

                    GINA (O.S)
          Gina Gambi. Newsroom

                    LISA
          Gina. Lisa. I just called Tony.
          Told me to eff off and put the
          phone down on me.

                    GINA (O.S)
          What else did you expect from the
          prick? Another conference, Lise?

                    LISA
          When?

                    GINA (O.S)
          Tomorrow evening? My place again?
          Same time?

                    LISA
          I'll be there. On the dot.

INT. NAKATA'S APARTMENT - NIGHT

Nakata drains full glass of whiskey on sofa, falls asleep.

DAY

Nakata awakes on sofa, gathers himself, enters his bedroom. From it come SOUNDS of a SHOWER.

LATER

Nakata, fully dressed, EXITS bedroom and apartment.

EXT. SLOVAK'S STUDIO WAREHOUSE - DAY

Nakata exits his black BMW SUV, enters building.

INT. SLOVAK'S STUDIO WAREHOUSE - DAY

Nakata takes elevator to studio. Slovak's waiting.

INT. SLOVAK'S STUDIO - DAY

Slovak's a man of few words. He leads Nakata to a sheeted painting on an easel.

                    SLOVAK
          You got the cash?

Nakata produces bundled $10,000. Slovak reaches for it.

                        NAKATA
            I'll see the painting first.

Slovak shows his fake, signed Fontana, two V-shape slashes, apart. Nakata studies it. Slovak gets impatient.

                        SLOVAK
            You can touch it; pick it up. I've
            dried it out.

                        NAKATA
              (admits)
            It's good.

                        SLOVAK
            It's back to fifteen.

                        NAKATA
            Ten.

Slaps money at Slovak who reflexively grabs it. Something about Nakata decides Slovak not to challenge him.

                        SLOVAK
            Take the fucking thing.

Nakata re-sheets painting. EXITS with it.

Slovak grabs pencil and paper, waits at window for Nakata to exit building, put painting in his SUV and drive off.

Slovak notes the license number: NEW YORK BCD-2145

EXT. NAKATA'S BROWNSTONE APARTMENTS HOUSE - DAY

Nakata parks outside, locks SUV, enters house with sheeted fake Fontana.

INT. NAKATA'S APARTMENT - DAY

Nakata enters. Black cell rings. Props fake Fontana against a wall. Answers cell.

                        NAKATA
            Karesa Agency.

The caller is SAUL BRAUNSTEIN, 55. Wealthy, arrogant.

                      BRAUNSTEIN (O.S.)
            I phoned you a minute ago. You didn't
            answer. You've been recommended to me.
            When and where can we meet?

                    NAKATA
          Alfredo's. Chelsea Market. One hour.

                    BRAUNSTEIN (O.S.)
          I would prefer somewhere less public.
          I suggest -

                    NAKATA
          One hour.
               (ends call)

INT. ALFREDO'S COFFEE SHOP, CHELSEA - DAY

Nakata and Braunstein, silver-haired, sit at a booth table.

Braunstein, conscious of meeting in public, hands a photo of
TRACIE, 20, to Nakata, who studies her open smile, questions
Braunstein with a look. He answers contemptuous, voice low.

                    BRAUNSTEIN
          She's a gold-digging tart who's
          seduced my son.

                    NAKATA
               (dislikes man's hauteur)
          I'd like to know more first.

                    BRAUNSTEIN
          He was all set to join the family law
          firm.
               (sneers)
          But she's bewitched him into thinking
          he's got a talent for art.

Incensed now.

                    BRAUNSTEIN (CONT'D)
          So much so he's enrolled. A *student!*
          Same college as *her*. She's even got
          him to move in with her. Using *his*
          trust fund, of course.
               (vicious)
          It's time for drastic measures.

Nakata hesitates, likes the look of Tracie, but then produces
his notebook.

EXT. ALFREDO'S COFFEE SHOP - DAY

Viewed through a window, Nakata jots Braunstein's replies in
his notebook, pockets it and Tracie's photo. EXITS.

Nods to O'Neill, walks off. Braunstein exits, looks about as
if fearful of being seen, hurries away. O'Neill follows him.

INT. NAKATA'S APARTMENT - NIGHT

Nakata pastes TRACIE WESTON copy-photo at TOP of Ledger page.

Black cell rings. O'Neill sends him Braunstein's photo, data. Nakata prints photo, pastes it on page, enters data and from his notebook: Braunstein's cell number. Adds PO Box number.

Dials Braunstein's cell. Braunstein answers, guarded.

> BRAUNSTEIN (O.S.)
> Saul Braunstein.

> NAKATA
> Karesa. Your PO box number is ...

EXT. A GREENWICH COFFEE SHOP - DAY

Greenwich's leafy streets are alive, shops open, pleasantries exchanged. Across the road from coffee shop is a small park.

Tracie sits at pavement table. Nakata sits at the next table, reading blurb of a DVD he's just bought.

It's a Glyndebourne edition of *Don Giovanni*. Black cover has Giovanni in black, holding Zerlina in a white wedding dress.

Nakata glances at art portfolio case by Tracie's feet. Asks.

> NAKATA
> Artist?

> TRACIE
> Student.

> NAKATA
> Really? I'm a lover of art. It's my overriding passion.

> TRACIE
> (pleasant)
> Any particular movement?

> NAKATA
> Impressionism. I'm also a great fan of Lucio Fontana.

> TRACIE
> One of the originators of spacialism. I rather like his work myself.

> NAKATA
> That's good to hear. I'm thinking of treating myself to one for sale in a local gallery. Except it's expensive.

                              TRACIE
                    I bet it is.

                              NAKATA
                    But what the hell. We only live once.
                    It's entitled Concetto Spaciale -

                              TRACIE
                    Aren't they all?

                              NAKATA
                    More specifically, his Attese, 1966.

                              TRACIE
                    With his inevitable slashes?

Nakata picks up on this opening.

                              NAKATA
                         (tad suggestive)
                    Of course. As any man who loves
                    women can't help but appreciate.
                    Symbolizing as they do -

Tracie cuts him off by smiling up at JOSH BRAUNSTEIN, 23.

                              TRACIE
                    You're late.

                              JOSH
                    Sorry, I was held up.
                         (grins)
                    But I ran all the way. If that will
                    get me back in your good graces.

                              TRACIE
                         (grips his hand)
                    You're never out of them.

Josh looks quizzically at Nakata.

                              TRACIE (CONT'D)
                    This is Mr - ?

                              NAKATA
                    Takashi. Simon Takashi.

                              TRACIE (CONT'D)
                    Mr Takashi's an art lover. More
                    especially, Lucio Fontana.

Josh indicates Nakata's DVD.

                              JOSH
                    I see you're also an opera lover,
                    Mr Takashi?

                    NAKATA
          Particularly *Don Giovanni* -

                     JOSH
               (cuts across him)
          I'm sorry, Mr Takashi, I don't mean
          to be rude.
               (to Tracie)
          If we don't want to miss the lecture,
          Trace, we have to be off.

Tracie glances at her wristwatch.

                    TRACIE
          Goodness, is that the time?

Stands, picks up her portfolio, smiles at Nakata.

                    TRACIE (CONT'D)
          Nice to have met you, Mr Takashi.

He watches them cross the road hand in hand, run through the park, clearly in love. Recalls Rachel and he being the same.

FLASHCUT: Rachel and he walk hand in hand through a park; kiss.

Tracie and Joshua pass from Nakata's view. He conflicts. Can he go through with this seduction?

INT. NAKATA'S APARTMENT - DAY

Nakata calls Braunstein's cell number. Braunstein answers.

                    NAKATA
          Karesa. It's NO.

Ends call, crosses out Braunstein's face, puts Ledger away.

INT. GINA'S APARTMENT - NIGHT

Holding a half full glass of wine, Gina tells Lisa more of what she knows of Anna's new man-friend.

                    GINA (CONT'D O.S.)
          She met him only the evening before.
               (expands)
          Tony promised to take her to an art
          exhibition but called off last minute
          and persuaded her to go on her own.

Gina tries to recall name of art gallery.

                    GINA (CONT'D)
          What was the gallery called ... ?

Gina remembers name of gallery.

> GINA (CONT'D)
> Monde! That was it! I remember it
> from a phrase, *mondo bizarrro,* my
> Mom used for something bizarre.
> It's in Greenwich.

Tops up both wine glasses. They clink them, toss wine down.
This could be the start of their quest to find the man.

INT. BRAUNSTEIN'S LUXURY PENTHOUSE - NIGHT

Braunstein sits at writing bureau. Dials out on landline a
number jotted on a note. His wife Leah, hard-faced, sits on
a sofa. A man answers the ringing tone.

> BRAUNSTEIN
> Your number's been given to me ...

INT. CHEAP BEDSIT - NIGHT

A MUGGER, 40, listens to Braunstein. Replies.

> MUGGER
> Ten grand, cash. Five up front.

> BRAUNSTEIN (O.S.)
> Wait on a moment.

INT. BRAUNSTEIN'S APARTMENT - NIGHT

Braunstein cups the phone, tells Leah the Mugger's terms.

> BRAUNSTEIN (CONT'D)
> Ten thousand? Half up front.

Leah nods, impassive. Braunstein replies to the Mugger.

> BRAUNSTEIN (CONT'D)
> How do I get the five to you?

Braunstein notes Mugger's instructions, replaces phone,
re-faces Leah. Die is cast.

INT. NAKATA'S APARTMENT - NIGHT

Fake Fontana hangs over mantelshelf, where Nakata can see
it from his sofa. There's no sign of picture it replaced.

Nakata brings up MEG's name on his LANDLINE, hesitates to
call it. His black cellphone rings. Answers it.

                    NAKATA (CONT'D)
          Karesa Agency.

INT. STUDY, HAGEN'S LUXURY APARTMENT - NIGHT

JAMES HAGEN, 45, a banker-type, talks low into study phone.

                    HAGEN
          You've been recommended to me. You
          run a ... a confidential service?

INT. NAKATA'S APARTMENT - NIGHT

Nakata switches off phone, turns to Rachel in portrait of
her with himself, almost pleads with her to understand.

                    NAKATA
          I have to, Rach. Having chosen my
          path, I've no alternative.

Surveys his luxurious room, his fine effects, especially
his "Fontana", challenges it all, broodingly, to himself.

                    NAKATA
          But is it worth it? Missing out on
          Emma's tender years?

INT. MONDE ART GALLERY - DAY

Lisa is indifferent to the yellow Fontana for sale, shows
Anna's photo to Monde, questions.

                    LISA
          It would have been a month ago at
          one of your evening exhibitions.

Monde's brusque reply betrays he recognizes Anna.

                    MONDE
          I'm sorry, madam. I can't possibly
          remember everyone who -

                    LISA
          She was with a man ...

INT. BEDROOM, HOTEL SUITE #3 - DAY

JULIA HAGEN, 40, gives Nakata lingering look, EXITS suite.
Nakata checks film has been recorded, starts dressing.

                    LISA (CONT'D O.S.)
          ... tall, dark hair, handsome.

INT. MONDE ART GALLERY - DAY

Lisa continues to question Monde.

                    LISA
          I was hoping he might be one of
          your regular clients?

A customer enters. It gives Monde an excuse to move away.

                    MONDE
          I'm sorry, madam, but no. Now if
          you'll excuse me.

Goes to customer. Lisa pockets Anna's photo. EXITS.

INT. NAKATA'S APARTMENT - NIGHT

Nakata sits at his laptop, bank account online, ledger open at Hagen's page, containing his and Julia Hagen's photos.

$25,000 enters his bank account. Nakata switches off laptop. Angrily scrawls PAID on page, places Ledger in drawer, bags a DVD to post.

On Nakata's coffee table is his *Don Giovanni* DVD. Inserts it in DVD player, forces himself to settle on sofa to watch it.

EXT. LEAFY STREET, GREENWICH - NIGHT

Tracie walks along a street carrying a bag of groceries and wearing shoulder bag. Hears footsteps, looks back, sees the MUGGER'S dark, hooded figure behind her.

Quickens her pace. So does Mugger. Ahead of her, Tracie sees her brownstone apartments house, drops groceries, runs.

Mugger comes up, knifes her, runs off with her shoulder bag. She staggers up steps, rings her apartment bell. Josh answers.

                    JOSH
          Welcome back to Shangri -

                    TRACIE
          Josh, I've been stabbed -

Collapses. Moments later, Josh opens door, kneels beside her.

INT. NAKATA'S APARTMENT - NIGHT

Nakata watches *Don Giovanni* DVD. Music is for Act 2, Scene 5. The setting: Don Giovanni's chambers.

Off stage, woman's scream is heard. Elvira enters on stage, flees through door. Giovanni tells Leporelli to look outside.

Leporelli runs back, in fear, into room, saying the Statue's appeared as promised. Ominous knocking sounds at the door.

Giovanni opens the door to Statue of Commendatore. It sings, gives Giovanni a last chance to repent.

     STATUE   TRANSLATION
 Don Giovanni! A cenar teco Don Giovanni! You invited
 m'invitasti -   me to dine with you -

Giovanni refuses to repent. The Statue sinks into the earth, takes Giovanni with it. A chorus of demons surround Giovanni as he's taken down to Hellfire.

The scene seems to upset Nakata. He stops the DVD, switches on the TV to a New York news channel.

On screen is BREAKING NEWS - a CRIME SCENE outside Tracie's brownstone apartments house.

DETECTIVE in charge of the case faces a barrage of questions, flashbulbs, from reporters, as he addresses TV cameras.

     DETECTIVE
 The victim was a twenty-year old
 art student living in Greenwich.
 Her name was Tracie Weston.
  (shows Tracie's photo)
 The attack appears to have been a
 mugging. If anyone knows anything,
 no matter how insignificant, that
 might assist our enquiries -

Nakata switches off TV, he knows who's responsible, buries face in his hands, shakes his head, "No. No."

INT. NAKATA'S APARTMENT - DAY

The table is now a SHRINE. Centred on it is Rachel and Emma's photo draped with black ribbon, with lighted Japanese tapers in holders on both sides. Table also has a kneeling stool.

Wearing a black robe, Nakats kneels before his shrine, looks up at painting of himself and Rachel, intones in Japanese.

     NAKATA   TRANSLATION
 Watashino ai no subete noeien My love will last for all
 no tsudhuku. Natashitachi mina eternity. Until we are all
 ga saikai sura made. Jyunsui reunited. In the Land of
 yorokobino tokore de.   Pure Bliss.

Bows low his shrine.

NAKATA (CONT'D)
Mou machigai wa kesu koto wa dekinai. Watishi ga dekiru koto ha tsugunai koto dake.

TRANSLATION
I cannot erase my wrongs. All I can do is atone.

Places Ledger on table, opens it at Braunstein's page. Offers a tanto on a Shinto sash to shrine.

NAKATA (CONT'D)
Watashino seishimo enchixoutoshite komo tanto seishen wona shimasu.

TRANSLATION
I name this tanto, seishen, as an extension of my spirit.

Lays sash and tanto on table. Focuses on Tracie's face.

NAKATA (CONT'D)
Anata wofuku shuushi masu. Watashiha futou na atsukaiwo motte subete no jixyosei.

TRANSLATION
I will avenge you. All the women I have wronged.

Nakata slices Braunstein's face.

NAKATA (CONT'D)
Starting with you, Braunstein. For Tracie Weston.

EXT. BRAUNSTEIN'S LUXURY APARTMENTS BLOCK - NIGHT

Nakata, in black, wearing gloves, hides by basement parking entrance. Door lifts for car. Nakata enters as door descends.

INT. BASEMENT, BRAUNSTEIN'S LUXURY APARTMENTS BLOCK - NIGHT

Nakata hides beside a vehicle. Car driver enters elevator. It ascends, stops at a floor.

Nakata calls elevator down. Ascends it to penthouse. Exits into its outer hallway.

Rings doorbell. Waits. Suspects Braunstein is studying him through security eye-viewer. Re-presses bell, holds it.

Braunstein's questions, aggressive, from inside.

BRAUNSTEIN (O.S.)
What do you want?

NAKATA
It's about Tracie Weston.

BRAUNSTEIN (O.S.)
What about her?

NAKATA
I know who you paid to kill her.

Braunstein remains silent.

                    NAKATA (CONT'D)
          I made him talk. But for a fee,
          I'll keep the police out of it.

Still silence from Braunstein.

                    NAKATA (CONT'D)
          I don't want to kick the door in.
          But if you force me to, I will.

Braunstein reluctantly opens door. Nakata enters.

INT. BRAUNSTEIN'S APARTMENT - NIGHT

Nakata enters inner hall, puts tanto to Braunstein's throat, forces him into sitting room.

Nakata sees Leah on sofa. He's momentarily surprised by her presence, flashes tanto to her throat, silencing any scream.

                    NAKATA
          I thought you lived alone.

Shoves Braunstein to sit with Leah who grabs at her husband's hand. He ignores hers, makes no attempt to allay her fear.

                    NAKATA (CONT'D)
          Your killer's contact number?

                    BRAUNSTEIN
          But you said –

Nakata flashes tanto back to Braunstein's throat. Leah moans, terrified. Braunstein indicates closed bureau.

                    BRAUNSTEIN
          Top drawer.

Nakata finds note with cell number, pockets it. Sees whiskey bottle on cabinet, gets two glasses, hands all to Braunstein.

                    NAKATA (CONT'D)
          Fill both up.

                    LEAH
              (voice trembles)
          I don't like whiskey.

                    NAKATA
          But you're going to drink it.
          You're now in this, too.

Braunstein fills the glasses.

                              NAKATA
                    Drink.

Braunstein downs his. Leah hesitates. Nakata puts tanto to
her throat. Forces her to drink. Nakata tells Braunstein.

                              NAKATA (CONT'D
                    Refill them.

LATER

Whiskey bottle's empty. Leah's almost comatose. Braunstein
is drunk but still thickly aware of what's happening.

Nakata produces new roll of cling-film bags from inside his
clothes, hands it to Leah. Unrealising what he wants her to
do with it, she takes it. Her prints are now on it. Nakata
gives it to Braunstein.

                              NAKATA (CONT'D)
                    Tear two off.

Also uncomprehending, Braunstein does so. Nakata puts cling
bags over their heads. Clawing at the bags, they smother to
death. Nakata clasps their hands together. Suicide pact. He
leaves cling-film roll on the sofa. EXITS.

INT. BASEMENT, BRAUNSTEIN'S LUXURY APARTMENTS BLOCK - NIGHT

Nakata exits elevator at basement parking, waits in shadows
by entrance door. Car enters. Nakata EXITS into the night.

EXT. DARK ALLEY #1 - NIGHT

Nakata appears out of the night, gets into his parked SUV.

INT. NAKATA'S SUV - NIGHT

Nakata dials number on Braunstein's note. Mugger answers.

                              NAKATA
                    I've a job needs doing yesterday.
                    Top dollar. Where can we meet?
                              (Mugger replies)
                    I know it. Wear something for me
                    to know you.
                              (Mugger replies)
                    Hooded jacket? Fine.

EXT. DARK ALLEY #2 - NIGHT

Nakata waits in his SUV, engine on. Man enters alley.

32

Nakata switches on headlights, sees man has hood up, drives SUV at him. Mugger runs, can't outpace SUV, presses himself against a wall. Nakata crushes him. Speeds off.

Switches on CD in his player. Music is from *Don Giovanni*.

INT. OPERA HOUSE - NIGHT

Positioned TV cameras show *Don Giovanni* is being televised.

Music is for the Cemetery Scene. Act 2, Scene 3.

On stage, Giovanni and Leporello are by Commendatore's tomb and Statue. Giovanni laughs. Statue warns him his laughter will not last beyond sunrise.

Nakata sits in the stalls, gripped by the opera.

INT. LISA'S APARTMENT - NIGHT

Lisa searches TV channels for something to occupy her mind. Stops on *Don Giovanni* opera.

Main TV camera is focused on the stage where:

Leporelli reads to Giovanni the inscription on statue's base.

LEPORELLI	TRANSLATION
Dell'empio che me trasse al passo estremo qui attende la vendetta.	I am waiting for revenge against the sacriligeous one who gave me death.

Another TV camera sweeps audience, pauses on Nakata who sees camera is on him, shields his face as if to focus on opera.

Camera moves away. Lisa switches to another channel.

INT. OPERA HOUSE - NIGHT

On stage, a chorus of demons surround Giovanni as he's taken below by Commendatore's statue to Hellfire.

Nakata is gripped as a Finale ensemble sings opera's moral.

ENSEMBLE	TRANSLATION
Quest e il fin di chi fa mal, e de'perfidi la morte alla vita e sempre ugual.	Such is the end of the evildoer, the death of a sinner always reflects his life.

LATER

Nakata broods in empty theatre. Undertones to himself.

                              NAKATA
                    I'd no choice. Having seen my
                    face, she had to die.

Usher comes to his row, waits for him to go. Nakata EXITS.

INT. NAKATA'S SHRINE - NIGHT

Nakata kneels, black-robed, Ledger open at faces of JAMES
and JULIA HAGEN. His avenging for the women he has wronged
is going to be last in, first out.

            NAKATA   TRANSLATION
    Watashino samurai no sosenno   In the way of my samurai
    honhoude. Ima watashino   forefathers. Now begins
    shoukan wokaishi shimasu.   my redemption.

Nakata raises tanto, recites a *haiku*.

            NAKATA   TRANSLATION
    Kore ga wagamichi. Watishi   This is my road.
    nomi ga iku koto ga dekiru.   Only I can take it.
    Mou moduru kotow a dekinai.   There is no turning back.

Slits Hagen's face.

INT. NAKATA'S APARTMENT - DAY

Wearing black, Nakata transfers bulk of his money online to
a MEG NAKATA bank account. Pockets tanto. EXITS.

INT. SLOVAK'S STUDIO - DAY

Slovak dials out. A voice answers. Slovak questions:

                    SLOVAK
              How much to trace a vehicle?
                    (voice answers)
              Three hundred. Fine.

INT. NAKATA'S APARTMENT - DAY

Seen through a window, Nakata drives away in his SUV.

                    SLOVAK (O.S.)
                (gives vehicle details)
              BMW SUV. New York, BCD 2145.

EXT. FINANCIAL DISTRICT, NEW YORK - DAY

Hagen exits with brief case from a building, walks off.

Nakata emerges from cover. He tails Hagen to Fulton Street subway station. They descend the steps.

INT. FULTON STREET SUBWAY STATION - DAY

Hagen passes through ticket barrier. Nakata follows as they descend the escalator.

INT. UPTOWN PLATFORM, FULTON STREET - DAY

Hagen enters onto the platform, waits near its edge. Nakata stands behind him as more commuters jostle around them.

SOUND of an incoming train is heard. Nakata nudges Hagen on to the rails just as train exits tunnel.

Yells. Screams. Panic. Confusion. Nakata walks away.

INT. NAKATA'S SHRINE - DAY

Ledger is open at BOB WARNER's page. His face is slit.

INT. INNER HALL, WARNER'S LUXURY APARTMENT - DAY

Open door to bedroom shows packing cases half-filled with Susan's clothes. More clothes are strewn about the room. Warner's smug voice on phone comes from sitting room.

> WARNER (O.S.)
> She'll be gone today, babe. You
> can move in any time after that.

Apartment's outer door slowly opens.

INT. SITTING ROOM, WARNER'S LUXURY APARTMENT - DAY

Warner hears outer door being closed, lowers voice.

> WARNER (CONT'D)
> She's back. Had to leave the door
> open for her. But I took her key.

Ends the call. Nakata enters the room, gripping tanto.

> WARNER (CONT'D)
> Hey! What the fuck -

Backs away in fear from Nakata toward open patio window.

> WARNER (CONT'D)
> This is my private apart-

Nakata puts tanto to Warner's throat. Warner looks at it in horror, blusters, all brashness gone.

                    WARNER (CONT'D)
    If this is about me disputing your
    fee -

                    NAKATA
    This is about you paying for what
    you did to your wife.

                    WARNER
    Me! What about *her*! *She's* the one
    that opened her legs -

                    NAKATA
      (slaps him hard)
    You drove her to it.

Nakata forces Warner out on to the patio.

                    NAKATA (CONT'D)
    She was just looking for affection.
    Which I doubt she ever got from you.

                    WARNER
    Yeah? That's because I was too much
    for her. She couldn't keep up -

Nakata slaps Warner again, forces him back to patio rail. Warner glances over his shoulder at the drop below.

                    WARNER
      (panics)
    This is fucking crazy, man. Let's
    go back inside and -

Nakata lifts Warner over rail by his ankles, doesn't look down after the falling man, pockets his tanto, re-enters sitting room and through to:

INNER HALL

Outer door starts to open. Nakata enters nearest room, a WC, leaves door cracked open, peers through and sees:

Susan enter, no make-up, loaded with small items for her move. Closes outer door behind her.

Susan senses the silence, is instantly edgy. Looks around, nervous, cautiously enters her bedroom, unloads her goods.

Nakata exits WC and EXITS apartment.

Susan exits bedroom still uneasy, locks outer door, checks kitchen and other rooms, enters sitting room.

INT. SITTING ROOM, WARNER'S LUXURY APARTMENT - DAY

Susan hears police and ambulance sirens, exits to patio.

She peers over the rail. Below her she sees body sprawled on sidewalk, surrounded by people, police, paramedics.

Even from a height, Susan sees it's Warner's body. Stares back into sitting room. *Did* she hear something?

She looks back over patio rail, sees man exit front doors of the apartment block. He looks familiar.

Man turns his face, calls a cab. Susan sees it's Nakata, steps back startled, returns to rail, sees cab drive away.

INT. OUTER HALLWAY, FALCO'S APARTMENT - DAY

Lisa rings Falco's doorbell.

INT. FALCO'S APARTMENT - DAY

Falco sees Lisa in door eye-viewer. Demands, aggressive.

>   FALCO
>   What do you want?

>   LISA
>   Talk.

>   FALCO
>   Fuck off.

INT. OUTER HALLWAY, FALCO'S APARTMENT - DAY

Lisa rings again, holds bell down.

>   FALCO (O.S.)
>   I said fuck off.

Apartment door down Hall opens. KATE HART, 45, beckons Lisa. Lisa enters apartment. Kate hugs her, shuts door.

INT. KATE HART'S APARTMENT - DAY

>   KATE
>   Oh, Lisa, what can I say? Anna was
>   was one of my dearest friends.

>   LISA
>   There's nothing to say Kate. Unless
>   you can tell me why she did it?

Kate takes Lisa through to her sitting room. They sit.

> KATE
> I'm sorry, Lisa, I can't. Except she was desperately unhappy with Tony.

> LISA
> Yes, but then she wrote me, saying she'd met someone?

> KATE
> I know. Came to tell me about him next day. She was over the moon. They met at an art exhibition -

> LISA
> (impatient)
> I know that much, Kate. It's the man I'm interested in.

> KATE
> I can't help you, Lisa ...

Adds, with no choice but to tell this:

> KATE (CONT'D)
> Except, it seems they instantly connected, went back to his hotel and ... well ... ended up in bed.
> (anxious to reassure Lisa)
> But *promising* to meet Anna again. Made her give him her cell number -

> LISA
> (cuts in, bitter)
> Except, he didn't call? For him it was just a one night -

> KATE
> (rushes to tell more)
> No, it was worse than that. She came running here next day in tears. It was a set-up. Tony paid the guy to seduce her, and *film* it, then send him a copy.

Sees the shock this is to Lisa, lets her absorb it.

> KATE (CONT'D)
> He gave her a day to clear out, with no divorce settlement, or he'd put it on the internet for all to see.

> LISA
> (vicious)
> The bastards. The bastards. Both.

                    KATE
              (stifles tears)
          Next thing I knew she'd taken an
          overdose. And was taken away in a
          body-bag.

Lisa's steely resolve returns, waits for Kate to recover.

                    LISA
          Anna gave me only his first name.
          Matthew. But did she tell you his
          surname? Or anything about him.

                    KATE
          Like you, nothing more than his
          first name. Oh, and that he had
          a thing about some painter ...

Struggles to bring it back to mind.

                    KATE (CONT'D)
          What's his name ... ? Yes, that
          was it. Fontana. Lucio Fontana.
          Rhymes with Montana, where I was
          born.

INT. NAKATA'S SHRINE - NIGHT

Nakata's Ledger is open, showing DAVID's and GRACE PERRY's faces. David Perry's face is slit.

EXT. DILAPIDATED RIVERSIDE WAREHOUSE - NIGHT

Perry drives an expensive car into warehouse's parking lot. Nakata sits in the rear, leaning forward over Perry.

INT. PERRY'S CAR - NIGHT

Nakata wears gloves, holds tanto to side of Perry's neck. He indicates river's edge, near a ramshackle pier.

                    NAKATA
          Park there.

Perry does so, fearing what comes next.

                    PERRY
              (pleads)
          Please, can't we discuss this?

Nakata produces a pistol, shoots Perry in the right, front side of stomach. Nakata grips Perry's right hand around the butt. Perry's arm falls away, gun drops to the floor.

Nakata peels off his bloodied right glove, inside out, opens door with gloved left hand, exits car, closes door.

EXT. DILAPIDATED RIVERSIDE WAREHOUSE - NIGHT

Nakata pockets gloves and tanto, walks off into the night.

INT. NAKATA'S APARTMENT - NIGHT

Nakata kneels at his shrine, holds up tanto in both hands, bows, replaces tanto on sash on the table, intones.

NAKATA	TRANSLATION
Shoukanno watashino tabiwot-sudhukete I masu -	My journey of redemption continues -

Doorbell rings. Nakata hesitates. It rings again, insistent. Nakata peers into door's eye-viewer. Sees Slovak. Opens door.

Slovak enters, all bravado, past Nakata.

SLOVAK
The guy below let me in.

Sees fake Fontana on wall.

SLOVAK (CONT'D)
Looks great there. I dare anyone to say it's not a Fontana.

Nakata waits for him to say what he's here for. Not sensing Nakata's menace, Slovak turns to portrait of Rachel/Nakata.

SLOVAK (CONT'D)
Your wife? Good looking broad.
    (picks up framed photo)
Cute looking kid, too.
    (fingers black ribbon)
But looks like you lost them both.
Sad. You must miss them.

Looks around apartment.

SLOVAK (CONT'D)
Great place you have here. Musta set you back plenty.

Thinking he's in control, Slovak wanders to the desk.

SLOVAK (CONT'D)
Guess you're wondering how I found you? And what I'm here for?

NAKATA
The what will suffice.

Slovak now senses Nakata's menace, gets edgy.

SLOVAK
The Fontana I did for you –

NAKATA
The fake.

SLOVAK
I was thinking I gave it away. And seeing how you live, I'm sure of it.

NAKATA
How sure?

SLOVAK
Say the extra five grand?

NAKATA
Let's not even say it.

SLOVAK
What! With all that's in here!

Checks desk. Nakata's eyes fix on his Ledger left on it.

SLOVAK (CONT'D)
This desk alone musta cost a mint.

Picks up Ledger, feels its leather cover.

SLOVAK (CONT'D)
And this feels the real thing.

Reads a page, realizes book could be dynamite.

SLOVAK (CONT'D)
Well, well. What have we here?

Flicks through more photos and data.

SLOVAK (CONT'D)
Looks like a shakedown book.

Nakata stays silently menacing.

SLOVAK (CONT'D)
Nothing to say? That confirms it. We got some re-negotiating to do, *Mr. John Nakata*.
    (turns the screw)
Yeah. I know your moniker, too, as well as your address.
    (gloats)
Which stacks the deck even more in my favor.

                    NAKATA
          By how much?

                    SLOVAK
          T*en* grand? Makes a nice round sum,
          don't you think?

                    NAKATA
          When?

                    SLOVAK
          Noon tomorrow.

                    NAKATA
          Where?

                    SLOVAK
          My place.

                    NAKATA
          I'll be there.

Slovak's eyes narrow, wary how easily Nakata's given in.

                    NAKATA (CONT'D)
          Let yourself out.

Still suspicious, Slovak EXITS.

Nakata kneels at shrine. Violently stabs tanto into table, removes his hand. Tanto quivers.

INT. NAKATA'S SHRINE - DAY

Ledger is closed on table. Tanto has gone.

INT. SLOVAK'S STUDIO - DAY

Slovak works on a fake painting. More are propped against a wall. Elevator rises, stops. Nakata exits, wearing gloves.

                    SLOVAK
          You're early. I was -

Nakata puts tanto to Slovak's throat, forces him back to the other stacked fakes. Slovak's shit scared.

                    SLOVAK (CONT'D)
          Listen, forget the money -

Nakata slits Slovak's throat, left to right. Slovak slides down wall into sitting position with his fakes. Nakata grips Slovak's right hand on tanto's hilt, lets it fall to floor, peels off bloodied gloves inside out, pockets them. EXITS.

EXT. BROOKLYN BOTANICAL GARDENS - DAY

Nakata strolls along a cherry blossom esplanade. Ahead, a BOY, 4, holds hands with Japanese man and Caucasian woman.

Boy glances back at Nakata.

Nakata flashbacks to when *he* was there as a little boy.

FLASHBACK

Nakata, 4, walks along the esplanade, holding hands on his left, with Japanese father, white-American mother on right.

They reach end of esplanade. Father wants to go left, mother wants to go right. He's pulled between them.

Mother gives in with a laugh. They follow Nakata's father.

BACK TO PRESENT DAY

Boy and his parents reach end of esplanade and go right.

Nakata turns left for the Japanese Hill-and-Pond Garden.

He strolls its winding paths, past artificial hills, trees and shrubs in bloom, to a Shinto shrine.

Stands at the foot of steps leading to the shrine, bows to it, continues on.

He reaches a pond with wooden bridges and man-made island, and a waterfall, where it tumbles into a small pool.

Nakata sees Rachel's face reflected in the pool. The sound of the falls becomes her laughter. Reaches out his hand to touch her, disturbs pool's surface. Her face ripples away.

EXT. JAPANESE SECTION, MOUNT OLIVET CEMETERY - DAY

Nakata, holding sprigs of white cherry blossom, kneels by Rachel's grave. Inset in black marble headstone is Rachel's photo. The wording on the stone reads:

    RACHEL NAKATA
      Aged 30
最愛の妻と一緒に大事にされた母
すべての永遠のとても気に入りました

A beloved wife and cherished mother
    Loved for all eternity

Nakata arranges his cherry blossom, talks to Rachel.

                    NAKATA
          Sakura, sakura, mi-watasu kagari

Nakata caresses Rachel's face, says it in English.

                    NAKATA (CONT'D)
          A mass of white blossom, as far as
          your eyes can see, Rach.

Reverts again to Japanese.

                    NAKATA (CONT'D)
          Mono no aware.
              (back to English)
          For the transcience of things.

Adds a white rose, which was under the blossom.

                    NAKATA (CONT'D)
          Shikashi watashino ai haeien ni
          tsudhuku.
              (again caresses her face)
          But my love will last for all of
          eternity.

Kneels back on his heels, pledges to her.

                    NAKATA (CONT'D)
          And when I've achieved my redemption,
          Emma and I can be together again.

Kneels, head bowed, as a late afternoon sun reddens the
sky. Rises, makes for his SUV.

EXT. ROMAN CATHOLIC SECTION, MOUNT OLIVET CEMETERY - DAY

Lisa lays pink roses on recently filled grave with wooden
cross and brass plate. It reads:

ANNA FALCO
   Aged 28

                    LISA
          I'll find him, Anna, I swear. And
          when I do I'll make them both pay.
          Him. And Tony.

Kisses her fingers, touches Anna's name, crosses herself,
rises, walks to her car, drives off.

EXT. MOUNT OLIVET CEMETERY - DAY

Nakata's SUV and Lisa's car come from separate directions,
both making for Main Exit.

Nakata reaches Exit first. Lisa tucks in behind him. Both exit right into Eliot Avenue.

INT. LISA'S CAR - DAY

Lisa follows Nakata along Eliot Ave. He continues along it for New York. She turns right into Fresh Pond Road for Queens.

INT. NAKATA'S SHRINE - NIGHT

Nakata kneels, offers up a NEW tanto.

NAKATA	TRANSLATION
Watashino shoukanni kono atarashi tanto wosaseguru. Watashiha watshino tamashii. No enchixy outoshite Tamashii no namae simashu.	I dedicate this new tanto to my redemption. I name it *Tamashii*. As an extension of my soul.

Lays tanto on sash, bows, remains in contemplation.

INT. NAKATA'S SHRINE - DAY

Ledger is open at CARL and AVA TORRES. Carl's face is slit.

INT. LISA'S APARTMENT - DAY

Lisa enters, reading an article in a newspaper, headlined:

FONTANA FAKER'S FATAL FINALE
    Slits Own Throat

She switches laptop on. Googles: fontana paintings, new york, is offered a number of museums and galleries. Among them are:

-- Guggenheim Museum -- with illustrated pages on Fontana

An illustration of a yellow Fontana, stirs Lisa's memory.

FLASHBACK: MONDE ART GALLERY

On the wall behind Monde as she shows him Anna's photo, Lisa sees a similar yellow Fontana on display.

BACK TO PRESENT:

Lisa switches off laptop, EXITS her apartment.

EXT. LARGE WOODED AREA, UPPER NEW YORK STATE - DAY

Nakata, wearing gloves, drives TORRES'S SUV along a track.

Next to Nakata is Torres, 35, drunk, and empty vodka bottle.

Nakata sees ideal spot. A stone bridge with parapet, over a stream, and branch hanging over it from leafless dead tree.

Drives on to bridge, cuts engine, exits SUV.

Nooses one end of a new rope, throws it over branch, opens Torres' door, puts it around Torres' neck, yanks him out of SUV by other end of the rope.

Lifts Torres over parapet. Lowers him so his feet are just level with top of parapet.

Torres swings to and fro clawing at the noose, feet kicking to try to land them on parapet, but can only scrape it.

Nakata tethers rope. Shuts passenger door. Leaves driver's door open. Walks off.

Torres' struggles stop. Dangles a few feet from parapet.

INT. MONDE ART GALLERY - DAY

Lisa enters, sees another painting has replaced the Fontana.

Monde is reading about Slovak's death in a newspaper. Lisa approaches him. He hurriedly tosses newspaper aside.

Monde recalls he's seen Lisa before, but bluffs it.

> MONDE
> Yes, madam?

Lisa re-shows him Anna's photo. Monde glances at it, wary.

> LISA
> I was here the other day, asking about my sister.

> MONDE
> I remember, but as I said then -

> LISA
> My call was more to do with the man she was with that night.

> MONDE
> My answer would have been the same. I can't possibly remember everyone who -

> LISA
> He was an art lover? Tall and dark as I previously described him.

Lisa stresses.

>   LISA (CONT'D
>   With an affinity for Fontanas?

Monde remains edgy. Lisa glances at the new painting.

>   LISA (CONT'D)
>   I see yours has gone?

Monde stays silent. Lisa indicates discarded newspaper.

>   LISA (CONT'D)
>   I also see you're reading about
>   the forger who killed himself?

>   MONDE
>   (forces his reply)
>   Yes. A dreadful business.

>   LISA
>   He specialized in Fontanas.

>   MONDE
>   So the paper says.

>   LISA
>   You wouldn't happen to have known
>   him by any chance?

>   MONDE
>   (blusters)
>   A forger. Definitely not. May I ask
>   what all this is about?

>   LISA
>   Just that I'm looking, as I said,
>   to find a man with an affinity for
>   Fontanas, and following every -

>   MONDE
>   I assure you there's no connection
>   between myself and a forger. Or the
>   man who -

Stops himself before he says too much. Lisa picks up on his sudden break.

>   LISA
>   The man who what, Mr Monde?

>   MONDE
>   (blusters)
>   The man you're looking for.

Lisa's tone now holds a threat.

                    LISA
          Maybe I should've mentioned, Mr
          Monde. I was once a Marine, and
          trained to break every bone in
          your body.

Monde sees Lisa means it, but still hesitates.

                    LISA (CONT'D)
          All I need is his name.

                    MONDE
          Yes, okay, I know him. But only
          slightly.

                    LISA
          His name?

                    MONDE
          I regret I don't know it.

                    LISA
          Then a fuller description?

                    MONDE
          Nothing more than you've said.

Lisa steps nearer, intimidating. Monde backs away.

EXT. TRAIN COMPARTMENT   DAY

Nakata looks out of window as train speeds for New York.

                    MONDE (CONT'D O.S.)
              (blurts)
          Except he's part Japanese.

EXT. MONDE'S ART GALLERY - DAY

Lisa exits. Stands on sidewalk, dials out on her cell. Gina Gambi replies to the usual background newsroom sounds.

                    GINA (O.S.)
          Gina Gambi. Newsroom.

                    LISA
          Did Anna say he was Japanese?

                    GINA (O.S.)
          No. What makes you ask that?

                    LISA
          I'll tell you later. Can you get
          me a phone number?

48

                    GINA (O.S.)
          Sure. Name? Address?

                    LISA
          Kate Hart. Same apartment block
          as Tony Falco.

Waits for Gina's reply. Notes it on back of hand. Clears
her line. Calls the number. Cuts across Kate Hart's voice.

                    LISA
          Kate, it's Lisa. Did Anna mention
          the guy's part Japanese?

                    KATE (O.S.)
          No. Was he?

Lisa's not in the mood to explain.

                    LISA
          Sorry, Kate. I have to go.

Cuts the call, walks off, wipes off Kate's number.

INT. LISA'S CAR - DAY

Lisa drives, deep in thought, through Greenwich, sees she's
nearing her church. On an impulse, she stops, enters it.

INT. ROMAN CATHOLIC CHURCH, GREENWICH - DAY

Lisa enters a pew, kneels, looks up at the Crucified Christ,
closes her eyes in silent prayer.

O'Donnell sees her from the chancel, sits in pew in front of
her. Lisa senses him. He waits for her to speak.

                    LISA
          Father, I've found out more about
          Anna. May I talk with you?

LATER

Lisa concludes to O'Donnell in a low voice, for a few others
praying nearby not to overhear.

                    LISA
          Tony paid him to film them.

                    O'DONNELL
          And now you've discovered he's -

                    LISA
          Part Japanese.

O'Donnell assimilates this.

                        O'DONNELL
Then, I regret to say, Lisa, it's possible he was a professional.

                        LISA
A professional?

O'Donnell expands on this.

                        O'DONNELL
The name given to them in Japan is *Wakaresaseya*. Translated, it means "breaker-uppers". Of marriages.

Hesitant to go on with this, but does so.

                        O'DONNELL (CONT'D)
I served my early years as a priest in Tokyo. There, *Wakaresaseaya* are a peculiar Japanese idiosyncrasy.

Hesitates again, then continues, condemnatory.

                        O'DONNELL (CONT'D
Conducting a very sordid profession.

Lisa waits for him to elaborate. He does, reluctantly.

                        O'DONNELL (CONT'D)
Japanese men who are paid to break up marriages by enticing wives into an ... an affair is the easiest way to describe it. And filming evidence for their husbands to divorce them.

Lisa starts to cut across him, but he concludes.

                        O'DONNELL (CONT'D)
For a pittance of a settlement. To prevent it being publicly shown for other people to witness their shame.

                        LISA
Poor Anna.

INT. NAKATA'S SHRINE - NIGHT

Ledger is open at EDWARD and OLIVIA COOPER - his face slit.

INT. LISA'S APARTMENT - NIGHT

Lisa enters, phones Gina.

                              GINA (O.S)
                    Gina Cambi -

                              LISA
                    It's me again, Gina. Sorry.

INT. BUSY NEWSROOM - NIGHT

Gina cradles her phone to her ear, busily typing with both
hands to a computer screen, desk littered with papers.

                              GINA
                    No need, Lise, it's quiet today.

                              LISA (O.S)
                    This morning's copy. An art forger
                    named Slovak slit his own throat?

                              GINA
                    This to do with Anna, too?

INT. LISA'S APARTMENT - NIGHT

Gina probes Lisa more.

                              GINA (CONT'D O.S.)
                    Earlier, it was her one-nighter
                    being Japanese. Now it's some guy
                    with a Polish name who's lopped
                    himself. What's the connection?

                              LISA
                    I'm not sure yet there is one.
                    But can you find out about him?

                              GINA (O.S.)
                    I'll get back to you.

EXT. CENTRAL PARK - NIGHT

BOY and GIRL walk through woods. Kiss. Over his shoulder she
sees Edward Cooper hanging on a rope from a tree; screams.

INT. NAKATA'S SHRINE - NIGHT

Nakata kneels, turns Ledger back a page to TONY FALCO, sees
Anna, who is just another wronged wife to him.

INT. NAKATA'S APARTMENT - NIGHT

Nakata watches DVD, its cover is on coffee table. Entitled:

51

VENGEANCE IS MINE
    A FILM BY
  SÔHEI IMAMURA

Cover shows a Japanese man, a killer, walking a city street, wearing a dark suit, dark glasses.

On TV screen, police corner him, there's no escape for him.

Nakata watches it, face inscrutable.

INT. NAKATA'S SHRINE - DAY

Ledger's still open at Tony Falco's page. His face is slit.

EXT. QUEENSBORO BRIDGE - DAY

The bridge has a low, early Sunday morning volume of traffic.

Like a zombie rendered inert, Falco doesn't resist as Nakata lifts him over pedestrian walkway rails into East River. Body goes under. Surfaces and swept away by fast-flowing current.

Nakata walks away. Keeps to Queens' side of the River, turns left into Vernons Blvd for the Noguchi Museum.

INT. LISA'S APARTMENT - DAY

Lisa sleeps, restless, in bed. Landline rings, she stretches for it, half asleep.

                   LISA
      Lisa Perano.

                 GINA (O.S.)
      The plot thickens, Lise.

Lisa sits up, fully awake now.

                 LISA
      Tell.

INT. BUSY NEWSROOM - DAY

                 GINA (CONT'D)
      Following on from you asking whether
      Anna's one-night stand was Japanese,
      guess what the Polish guy you're now
      interested in used to kill himself?

                 LISA (O.S.)
      No idea.

INT. LISA'S APARTMENT - DAY

                    GINA (O.S.)
          A Japanese tanto. So I'm thinking,
          slitting your own throat's drastic
          enough. But why would a Janislav
          Slovak, a Polish forger, use a
          ritual samurai dagger to do it?

                    LISA
               (brews on this)
          Gina, give me a moment to gather
          my thoughts; I'll get back to you.

INT. NOGUCHI MUSEUM - DAY

Nakata crosses the museum floor, enters the SCULPTURES HALL and goes straight to a sculpture of:

A man, twisted in an almost crucifixional shape, and a rope around his neck, encaged by four steel bars. Its title is:

DEATH (LYNCHED FIGURE) 1934

Nakata sits, broods at the sculpture.

INT. LISA'S APARTMENT - DAY

Deep in thought, Lisa drinks black coffee. Phone rings. She picks it up. Gina Gambi doesn't give her a chance to speak.

                    GINA (O.S.)
          Lise, the plot's thickening so fast
          it's getting to be as clear as mud.
          But bear with me as I lay it out.

INT. BUSY NEWSROOM - DAY

Gina studies data on her computer screen.

                    GINA
          In addition to Slovak; Mike, one of
          our crime guys, noticed the city's
          having a sudden spate of suicides.
          Other than a married couple, three
          in two days.

Reads out from her screen.

                    GINA (CONT'D)
               (stresses)
          All are wealthy men. Two business
          men. A banker. No money problems.

LISA (O.S.)
          Maybe they just got tired of the rat
          race. But what's this got to do with
          Anna -

                    GINA
          None of them left suicide notes.

INT. LISA'S APARTMENT - DAY

Lisa realizes that Gina hasn't finished, waits.

                    GINA (CONT'D O.S.))
          What's more, they were *all* on the
          point of swapping their wives for
          pastures new, and consequently no
          seeming reason to kill themselves.

                    LISA
          Something tells me you're not done?

                    GINA (CONT'D O.S.)
          Last night there were two more. One
          upstate. The other in Central Park.
          Both hung themselves. But in their
          cases, they'd already given their
          wives the heave-ho and moved their
          bimbos in.

INT. METROPOLITAN MUSEUM OF ART - DAY

Nakata walks to a painting: CRUCIFIXION (CORPUS HYPECUBUS) by Salvador Dali: Christ crucified to a Cross, suspended far above Earth on His way to Heaven, and Mary Magdalene looking up at Him.

                    LISA (O.S.)
          Carry on.

                    GINA (O.S.)
          Mike Googled them.

                    LISA (O.S.)
          And?

                    GINA (O.S.)
          There's a common pattern to them.

Gina stresses her punch line.

                    GINA (O.S. CONT'D)
          Japanese.

Nakata sits, broods up at the Crucifixion scene.

INT. LISA'S APARTMENT - DAY

Lisa asks Gina to expand on this.

                    LISA
          In what way exactly?

                    GINA (O.S.)
          Each death fits in with Japanese
          methods of committing suicide.

INT. BUSY NEWSROOM - DAY

Gina reads out from her computer screen.

                    GINA (CONT'D)
          Jumping in front of trains. Leaping
          off high places. Disembowelment. And
          though the one who did, blew his guts
          out with a pistol, which isn't quite
          the same, it's just as effective.

Gina returns to her screen.

                    GINA (CONT'D)
          Hanging ... that's another of their
          methods. Especially in wooded areas.
                    (stresses)
          As both men yesterday did.

INT. LISA'S APARTMENT - DAY

Lisa absorbs this. Gina cuts in on her thoughts.

                    GINA (O.S.)
          You ready to share all you've found
          out with me, Lise?

                    LISA
          Not quite yet, Gina.

                    GINA (O.S.)
          Tomorrow then? My place again?

                    LISA
          Sure, okay. But first, would you do
          me one more favour?

                    GINA (O.S.)
          Name it.

                    LISA
          Addresses, names, of the cast-off
          wives?

                    GINA (O.S.)
               I'll call you back.

INT. NAKATA'S APARTMENT - NIGHT

Nakata enters with two tube containers. Extracts illustrated copy-paintings, spreads them on coffee table. They are:

Noguchi's Death (Lynched Figure).
Dali's Crucifixion (Corpus Hypecubus).

Nakata sits, broods over them.

INT. LISA'S APARTMENT - NIGHT

Lisa snatches up her ringing phone, pen and paper ready.

                    LISA
               Gina?

INT. BUSY NEWSROOM - NIGHT

Gina refers to three names and addresses on note pad.

                    GINA
               I've only got the first three.
               I'll get you the others a.s.a.p.

INT. LISA'S APARTMENT - NIGHT

Lisa notes the three names, addresses.

                    LISA
               Thanks, Gina.

                    GINA (O.S.)
               Lise ...! Whatever's going on in
               your mind, give me some clue.

                    LISA
               Tomorrow, Gina.

Cuts call as Gina protests.

INT. NAKATA'S APARTMENT - NIGHT

Nakata broods over Dali's Corpus Hypecubus. Asks himself.

          NAKATA   TRANSLATION
     Watashi no michi wa tadashii   Is my way the right way?
     desk ka?

Nakata turns to Noguchi's Death (Lynched Figure), gets a:

VISION

The sculptured, distorted man, inside the cage is himself. He shakes the bars, trying to get free. More bars descend, enclosing him more. He's in HELL. Noose tightens about his neck. Choking, he claws at it.

END OF VISION

Nakata comes out of the vision, back to his apartment.

Looks at the illustration of Dali's Crucifixion, then at Death (Lynched Figure). Has he chosen the right path? He sweeps Christ off the table.

EXT. MEG'S HOUSE - DAY

The big clapboard house stands alone on a headland, on North Shore, Long Island, overlooking Long Island Sound. Meg and Emma walk hand in hand across the headland. Emma runs away, Meg chases her. Emma's laughter rings out as she runs.

INT. NAKATA'S SHRINE - DAY

Ledger is open at JAKE ROSS'S, 45, and MIA ROSS'S, 35, page. Jake's face is slit.

EXT. OUTER HALLWAY, PERRY'S LUXURY APARTMENT - DAY

Lisa rings bell. Grace Perry opens the door. Asks abruptly.

                GRACE
    Yes?

                LISA
    I'm trying to trace someone? A man,
    mid-thirties, part Japanese -

Grace slams door shut.

EXT. OUTER HALLWAY, HAGEN'S LUXURY APARTMENT - DAY

Julia Hagen is vitriolic to Lisa.

                JULIA
    Other than James doing me a big
    favour of falling under a train
    before I was forced to move out,
    I hope the Nip burns in Hell.
        (soundly shuts door)

EXT. DARK ALLEY #3 – DAY

Through his SUV window Nakata buys heroin and needle from a back-alley seller, drives off.

INT. OUTER HALLWAY, WARNER'S LUXURY APARTMENT – DAY

A MAID informs Lisa at the apartment door.

> MAID
> I'm afraid Mrs Warner is away.

> LISA
> When will she be back?

> MAID
> Late Wednesday. Is there a message?

> LISA
> It'll keep. I'll call back Thursday.

INT. JAKE ROSS'S LUXURY APARTMENT – DAY

Nakata threatens ROSS with his tanto, ties him in armchair with rope, but slack enough not to leave marks. Ross bucks in protest as Nakata produces a needle, injects heroin in Ross's arm. Ross goes into a coma, and will soon die.

Nakata grips Ross's hand on syringe, lets it drop, unties rope, EXITS with it.

INT. GINA'S APARTMENT - NIGHT

Gina repeats what Lisa's just told her.

> GINA
> So, Father O'Donnell thinks Tony may have hired a professional ...?

> LISA
> *Wakarasesaya* the Japanese call them.

> GINA
> Whatever. But Tony paid him to seduce Anna so he could divorce her for a zilch pay-off?

> LISA
> Except that Anna fell for him, but when she found out what he was and that he'd filmed all that happened between them, she couldn't take it and killed herself.

GINA
The creeps. Him and Tony both.

LISA
As one of the wives said to me, I hope they both burn in Hell.

GINA
But you had no luck with any of the three.

LISA
Two wouldn't speak to me, the other was away.

GINA
So, what makes you think this Waka guy could now be killing off their ex-husbands?

LISA
A gut feeling.

GINA
Based on him being Japanese and the deaths fitting some Shinto pattern?

Lisa nods.

GINA (CONT'D)
But what's his motive? His reason for killing them?

LISA
I don't know. Nor substantiate it.

GINA
It's a bit tenuous, don't you think?

LISA
Except, it's all I've got to go on.

GINA
In which case, shouldn't you tell the police your suspicions?

LISA
I doubt they'd listen. But if and when I get proof, I will.

Gina produces a note.

GINA
Then here's the details of the other two wives. But take care. If you're right, this guy's dangerous.

LISA'S APARTMENT - NIGHT

Lisa enters. Her phone rings. Answers it.

                    GINA (O'S)
          I'm beginning to think you're right,
          Lise.

                    LISA
          Another suicide?

                    GINA (O.S.)
          Yes. But prepare for a shock. It's
          Tony. He's been found, floating in
          Upper Bay. From the number of bones
          broken, they think it most likely
          he jumped off a high bridge.

                    LISA
          Gina, if anything could make my day
          at this moment, that would be it.

                    GINA (O.S.)
          I guessed you'd be pleased. Let me
          know how you get on today with the
          remaining wives. Or rather, widows.

                    LISA
          Sure, Gina.

Lisa ends call. Gets pistol from drawer. Aims it at display
plate on a wall, pulls trigger. CLICK. Pistol is empty.

INT. NAKATA'S SHRINE - DAY

Ledger is open at LUKE'S and ABBY VAN ALLEN'S page, both 40.
His face is slit.

INT. LISA'S APARTMENT - DAY

Lisa loads pistol, pockets it. EXITS

INT. OUTER HALLWAY, AVA TORRES' MODEST APARTMENT - DAY

Ava Torres replies to Lisa through half open door.

                    AVA TORRES (O.S.)
          No, I'm not willing to talk about
          him. Except I hope he gets caught
          and swung up by his dick for what
          he's reduced me to.

Shuts door.

INT. LUKE VAN ALLEN'S CAR - DAY

Car is stationary, engine off, at top of a slope leading down to a cliff at a lonely spot out in the country.

Van Allen sits behind the wheel, Nakata beside him, holding tanto to his throat. Nakata releases handbrake. Car slowly gathers speed as it rolls toward cliff-top.

EXT. CLIFF TOP - DAY

Nakata's flings himself out of car. It goes over the cliff on to rocks below, bursts into flames. Nakata walks off.

INT. OLIVIA COOPER'S MODEST APARTMENT - DAY

Olivia's willing to talk to Lisa. She's not long moved in.

                    OLIVIA
     He turned to me in Tiffany's where
     I was trying on a necklace. Told me
     I looked a million dollars with it.

Decides to confess all.

                  OLIVIA (CONT'D)
     He was years younger than Edward. I
     was flattered by his attention, and
     one thing sort of lead to another.
           (expands)
     He invited me to have coffee with
     him. In his hotel lounge ...

Hesitates, finds it difficult to say how easy she was.

                  OLIVIA (CONT'D)
     Next thing we were in his room. In
     bed.
           (justifies herself)
     Well, it was well over a year since
     Edward last came near me - And so,
     yes, I confess I was easy.
           (anger flares)
     Which I guess was what Edward had
     banked on - the sleaze. Next day
     he showed me a film of it ...

Buries her face in her hands, looks up.

                  OLIVIA (CONT'D)
     Everything that happened. In the
     most intimate detail.

Lisa gives her a moment, prompts her.

                    LISA
          Mrs. Cooper?

                    OLIVIA
               (gathers herself)
          The short of it is that rather than
          face a sordid divorce case with it
          all made public, and in the gossip
          columns for everyone to read.

Almost breaks down again.

                    OLIVIA (CONT'D)
          I settled for a fraction of what I
          was entitled to and moved *here*.

Looks angrily around room.

                    OLIVIA (CONT'D)
          For Edward to move a peroxide gold
          digger into my home. Half his age.
               (vengeful)
          Or *was*. Before he hung himself up
          on a goddam tree in Central Park.

Olivia adds, vicious.

                    OLIVIA (CONT'D)
          But why couldn't he have hung
          himself a week earlier? Before I
          signed the fucking papers.

Lisa stays discreetly silent.

INT. NAKATA'S SHRINE - DAY

Nakata opens DANIEL MARTINS, 34, page, studies his face.

INT. DANIEL MARTIN'S CAR - DAY

Daniel drives car through Long Island countryside, talking to his companion: Meg Nakata. They're clearly in love.

Daniel says something to Emma, sitting in the back. Emma heartily laughs. She's one very happy little girl.

INT. NAKATA'S SHRINE - DAY

Nakata poises his tanto over Daniel's face in his Ledger. Cell rings. Replaces tanto on Shinto sash, answers call.

                    NAKATA
          Karesa.

INT. O'NEILL'S DINGY APARTMENT - DAY

O'Neill, Nakata's PI, tells Nakata.

> O'NEILL
> Something urgent's come up.

INT. NAKATA'S APARTMENT - SAME TIME

Nakata replies to O'Neill.

> NAKATA
> Nico's Diner. One hour.

EXT. NICO'S DINER - DAY

Nakata reaches Diner, sees O'Neill sitting at secluded corner table inside, drinking coffee. Nakata enters.

INT. NICO'S DINER - DAY

Nakata sits opposite O'Neill, who's clearly edgy.

> O'NEILL
> Coffee?

> NAKATA
> You said it was urgent?

> O'NEILL
> I haven't heard from you for days.

> NAKATA
> I've retired.

> O'NEILL
> That's what I figured. You must have made a mint by now, huh?

> NAKATA
> Enough.

> O'NEILL
> I kinda figured that, too.

Nakata waits for O'Neill to get to the point.

> O'NEILL (CONT'D)
> I could do with a redundancy fund. Without your work, times could get hard.

Nakata never wastes time arguing.

                    NAKATA
          How much?

                    O'NEILL
          Say ten grand?

                    NAKATA
          Same time tomorrow.

                    O'NEILL
          Make it Charlie's. More friendly.

                    NAKATA
          Sure.

O'Neill watches Nakata EXIT - suspicious how easy it was.

INT. LISA'S APARTMENT - NIGHT

Lisa's phone rings. She picks it up. Gina gets in first.

                    GINA (O.S.)
          There's been two more.

INT. BUSY NEWSROOM - NIGHT

Gina details them to Lisa.

                    GINA
          One from an overdose of heroin. The
          other drove his car over a cliff.
          Both recently gave their wives the
          heave-ho. Again no suicide notes.

                    LISA (O.S.)
          He's keeping himself busy.

                    GINA
          You can say that again. Now makes
          eight in total. I've got you both
          wives' names and addresses.

INT. LISA'S APARTMENT - NIGHT

Lisa finds pen, paper, jots them down as Gina gives them.

                    LISA
          Thanks again, Gina.

INT. BUSY NEWSROOM - NIGHT

Gina has more to add.

                    GINA
          It's no longer your gut feeling,
          Lise. The police are now on to it.
          We have to tell them all we know.

INT. LISA'S APARTMENT - NIGHT

                    LISA
          Just let me talk to these two first,
          Gina? And the one who was out the
          day I called?

INT. BUSY NEWSROOM - NIGHT

Gina hesitates.

                    GINA
          I don't know, Lise.

                    LISA (O.S.)
          For Anna?

                    GINA
          Okay. I shouldn't, but okay. On
          condition ...

INT. LISA'S APARTMENT - NIGHT

Lisa anticipates Gina's condition.

                    LISA
          Whatever I find out, I share it
          with you first. Your scoop.

                    GINA (O.S)
          You've got it. Take care.

Lisa remembers something, calls down the phone.

                    LISA
          Gina!

Gina waits for Lisa to continue.

                    LISA (CONT'D)
          The suicide pact couple? Weren't
          they the first?

                    GINA (O.S.)
          As I remember.

                    LISA
          Did they leave a note?

                              GINA (O.S.)
                    I don't know. I'll check.

                              LISA
                    And whatever else you can find.

                              GINA (O.S.)
                    Will do. That it?

                              LISA
                    That's it.

                              GINA (O. S.)
                    I'll get back to you.

INT. CHARLIE'S HIVE INN - DAY

Nakata sits at quiet table. O'Neill enters, sits opposite.

                              O'NEILL
                    Got it?

Nakata hands him an envelope. O'Neill opens it.

                              NAKATA
                    It's all there.

                              O'NEILL
                    Don't doubt it. Just want to see
                    what ten grand looks like.

O'Neill glances at the money, stands, extends his hand.

                              O'NEILL (CONT'D)
                    Been good doing business with you.

Nakata doesn't take O'Neill's hand. O'Neill shrugs, EXITS.
Nakata waits a few moments then exits after O'Neill.

EXT. CHARLIE'S HIVE - DAY

Nakata searches street for O'Neill, no sign of him. Nakata
tries to guess which way he went, heads up street.

INT. CHARLIE'S HIVE - DAY

O'Neill re-enters through rear door, goes to front window,
watches Nakata go, returns to table, checks money.

INT. MIA ROSS'S MODEST APARTMENT - DAY

Lisa sits listening to Mia Ross.

                    MIA
          Other than his name's Mark, I know
          no more about him than you do.

                    LISA
          But your husband never took drugs?

                    MIA
          Jake? Never even smoked a cigarette.

INT. ABBY VAN ALLEN'S MODEST APARTMENT - DAY

Lisa sits listening to Abby.

                    ABBY
          Luke drive off a cliff? Never in a
          million years. He was terrified
          of heights.

Relates anecdote about Luke.

                    ABBY (CONT'D)
          A couple of years ago, on a trip
          to Paris, I got him to risk the
          Eiffel Tower. By the time we got
          to the top, and all those open
          girders, he was so shit-scared
          he sat on the elevator floor and
          wouldn't get out.

Comes back to now.

                    ABBY
          I told the police this and said
          Luke just couldn't have done it;
          but they said there was no other
          explanation.

INT. LISA'S APARTMENT - NIGHT

Lisa enters, feels low having made no progress. Idles
about, decides to call Gina.

                    GINA (O.S)
          Gina Cambi. Newsroom.

                    LISA
          I'm thinking of packing it all in,
          Gina. I'm making no progress.

INT. BUSY NEWSROOM - NIGHT

Gina's got news for Lisa.

                    GINA
          Don't give in yet. I checked
          out the Braunsteins. No note.

INT. LISA'S APARTMENT - NIGHT

Lisa listens as Gina continues.

                    GINA (CONT'D O.S.)
          But how about this connection?
          A well-known mugger was killed
          by a hit and run. And when the
          cops checked out his room, guess
          whose credit cards they found?

Stresses her own answer.

                    GINA
          Braunstein's son's girlfriend,
          who was mugged and killed the
          day earlier. His name's Joshua.
          Address is ...

Lisa notes down the address.

INT. NAKATA'S APARTMENT - NIGHT

Nakata sits, deep in thought. Illustrations of "Crucifixion (Corpus Hypecubus)" and "Death, Lynched Figure", are rolled up on the coffee table.

Nakata suddenly rises, goes to his shrine. Ledger is still open at Daniel Martins' face. Black cell rings again.

                    NAKATA
          Karesa.

                    O'NEILL
          O'Neill.

                    NAKATA
          Let me guess. Money was short?

                    O'NEILL
          Right on.

                    NAKATA
          By how much?

                    O'NEILL
          Five grand.

                    NAKATA
          Where?

                    O'NEILL
          Same place tomorrow. Same time.

INT. CHARLIE'S HIVE - DAY

O'Neill sits waiting, checks watch, dials Nakata's cell.

EXT. A DOORWAY, OPPOSITE CHARLIE'S HIVE - DAY

Nakata hides in a doorway watching the bar. Cell rings.

                    NAKATA
          Karesa.

                    O'NEILL (O.S.)
          You're late.

                    NAKATA
          I'm held up in traffic.

                    O'NEILL (O.S)
              (edgy at reply)
          How long?

                    NAKATA
          I couldn't even guess.

                    O'NEILL (O.S.)
          Can't wait. Same time tomorrow.

Cuts the call. Nakata waits.

O'Neill exits, looks about, heads up street. Nakata follows from distance. O'Neill often looks back, never sees Nakata.

INT. JOSH BRAUNSTEIN'S APARTMENT, GREENWICH - DAY

Lisa rings door bell, waits for door to open.

Josh stands aside listless, lets Lisa into apartment. He's unshaven, wears black, and black skull cap.

Framed photographs of Tracie, and Saul and Leah Braunstein, are draped in black ribbon. Mirrors are covered.

Josh indicates Lisa to a chair. She sits. He sits opposite. She glances at Tracie's photo.

                    LISA
          You must miss her?

                    JOSH
          Like crazy.

                    LISA
          I'm sure. I can empathize with the
          way you must be feeling. I've just
          lost my sister.

Lisa's reply suddenly puts Josh on his guard.

                    JOSH
          Aren't you from the police?

                    LISA
          Sorry, Josh, no. It's personal. I'm
          trying to trace a man who might have
          been involved in Tracie's death. Or
          rather, may have killed her mugger.

                    JOSH
          Killed her mugger? I don't understand?

                    LISA
          All I know about him is that he's
          part Japanese. And has a thing about
          an artist. Lucio Fontana.

                    JOSH
          But Trace and I met a man of that
          description only the other day -

Lisa cuts across him.

                    LISA
          Say that again, Joshua. You mean
          you've spoken to the guy?

INT. O'NEILL'S DINGY APARTMENT - DAY

O'Neill enters, closes Yale-lock door, peers out of window, still edgy that Nakata may have followed him.

INT. O'NEILL'S DINGY APARTMENTS BUILDING - DAY

Nakata reaches landing to O'Neill's apartment. But which is O'Neill's? He calls O'Neill's cell, hears it ring.

He goes to O'Neill's door, sees it has a Yale lock, opens it in a second with a plastic bank card.

INT. O'NEILL'S DINGY APARTMENT - DAY

O'Neill is switching off his cell as Nakata enters.

Nakata produces pistol with silencer. PHUT. Shoots O'Neill dead, pockets pistol and O'Neill's cell. EXITS, locks door.

INT. JOSH BRAUNSTEIN'S APARTMENT - DAY

Josh, shocked by Lisa's revelations, questions her more.

>   JOSH
> And you say that these Wakara - ?

>   LISA
> Get paid to break-up relationships.

>   JOSH
> But the only relationship broken
> up is mine and ...

Voice tails off as he suspects where this is leading, but still can't take in what Lisa's implying.

>   LISA
> Yes, Joshua. Yours and Tracie's.

Josh looks at Saul, Leah's photo, broods over it all.

>   JOSH
> They never accepted Tracie. Kept
> trying to split us.

Lisa spells out her known facts.

>   LISA
> Ruling out their deaths as suicide,
> they were the first to be killed.
> The mugger later, that same night.

Theorises her conclusion.

>   LISA (CONT'D)
> I think in some way, the catalyst
> for this man suddenly becoming a
> killer, was Tracie's death.

>   JOSH
>   (repeats)
> Tracie's death?

>   LISA
> I'm guessing here, Joshua, but I
> think your parents approached him
> to break you and her up. For some
> reason he refused, so they paid
> the mugger to -

Hesitates, not wanting to say it bluntly. But Josh says it for her, voice bitter as it dawns on him.

>   JOSH
> To kill her?

Lisa nods, continues.

                    LISA
          So, he killed them and the mugger
          in return.

                    JOSH
          To avenge her?

                    LISA
          Something like that.

                    JOSH
              (vicious)
          Then I'm glad he did.

Josh hurls parents' photo, it shatters. He's silent for
a moment, numb, absorbing it all, then questions Lisa.

                    JOSH (CONT'D)
          But why are you trying to find him?

                    LISA
          My sister's death was also caused
          by this same man.

                    JOSH
          I'm sorry, but other than he's in
          maybe his early-thirties, I can't
          tell you any more about him than
          you already know ...

INT. NAKATA'S APARTMENT - DAY

Nakata watches his *Don Giovanni* DVD. Its black cover, with
Don Giovanni carrying the bride, is on his coffee table.

The illustrations of Crucifixion (Corpus Hypecubus), and
Death (Lynched Figure) are also still on the table.

                    JOSH (CONT'D O.S.)
          ... except he's an opera lover.

Nakata's door-bell rings.

He pauses the DVD, hides the illustrations behind cushions
and answers door. It's Susan Warner.

He moves aside for her. She enters apartment, takes off her
coat, tosses it on chair. She's not the shy Susan of before.

She sees *Don Giovanni* on pause, picks up DVD cover.

                    SUSAN
          Reliving the evening we met?

                    NAKATA
          Yes, I was watching it.

Susan puts cover down.

                    NAKATA (CONT'D)
          How did you find where I lived?

                    SUSAN
          That night, after I left your hotel
          room, I waited outside in a cab.
                (hesitates to tell it)
          Then got the cabbie to follow yours
          here, paid him off and waited outside
          for your light to come on.

She rushes an admission.

                    SUSAN (CONT'D)
          I've never done anything like that
          before in my life. But I wanted to
          see where you lived. I watched you
          move about inside for a while, then
          took another cab home.

Looks into Nakata's eyes.

                    SUSAN (CONT'D)
          Why? Why did you do it to me?

                    NAKATA
          It's what I am.

                    SUSAN
          No, there was more than that between
          us. That evening. In your hotel room.

                    NAKATA
          I have to keep my emotions separate.

                    SUSAN
          But you didn't. I felt it.
                (begs him to admit it)
          I was more than just an assignment
          to you? Wasn't I?

                    NAKATA
                (can't deny it)
          If circumstances were different.

                    SUSAN
          Circumstances?

She looks around apartment, sees Japanese style painting
of Nakata and Rachel above shrine. Crosses to it, picks up
framed photo of Rachel and Emma, takes in the black ribbon.

                    SUSAN
          Your wife?

Nakata nods.

                    SUSAN (CONT'D)
          How did she die?

                    NAKATA
          Cancer.

                    SUSAN
          And your daughter?

Nakata is reluctant to talk about his private life.

                    NAKATA
          She's now five.

Susan glances toward bedrooms.

                    NAKATA (CONT'D)
          She lives with my sister.

                    SUSAN
          You must miss her?

Nakata's silence is his reply. She suddenly asks him.

                    SUSAN (CONT'D)
          Why did you kill my husband?

Nakata is caught out by the question.

                    SUSAN (CONT'D)
          I saw you leave the apartment.

Nakata asks sotto voce, a touch of menace to it.

                    NAKATA
          Have you told anyone?

                    SUSAN
              (meets his eyes)
          No.

                    NAKATA
          Are you intending to?

                    SUSAN
          No.

She takes his hands. He fights temptation to hold her. She senses his turmoil. A long moment passes ...

Nakata disengages her hands, gives her her coat.

                    NAKATA
          Then we should leave it at that.

                    SUSAN
          No. That's not the end of it. You
          know it's not.

She puts on her coat.

                    SUSAN (CONT'D)
          I'll be there for you should you
          decide.

Picks up DVD cover, hands it to Nakata face up, with Don Giovanni carrying the bride in her white gown.

                    SUSAN (CONT'D)
          Think of me some more.

EXITS. Nakata stands there, no clue to what he's thinking.

INT. WARNER'S LUXURY APARTMENT - NIGHT

Susan enters, turns on Hall lights, shuts outer door and enters bedroom. SOUNDS of her moving about come from room.

Nakata enters, closes outer door, enters sitting room.

Susan exits bedroom, locks outer door, switches off Hall lights, re-enters bedroom. Its light goes out. Apartment is in darkness. Silent.

LATER

Nakata exits sitting room, quietly enters Susan's room.

INT. SUSAN'S BEDROOM - DAY

Some instinct wakes up Susan. Sees Nakata's *Giovanni* DVD on her bedside table, cover facing her.

It takes a moment for this to register. She springs out of bed, exits bedroom, checks outer door is locked.

Enters sitting room. Empty. Checks other rooms, returns to bedroom. Exits with DVD, re-enters sitting room.

Sits, mulls over DVD, looks past patio at city beyond.

INT. NAKATA'S SHRINE - DAY

Nakata kneels, black robed, re-looks at Martins' photo. eyes move to Martins' wife, DEBRA, 38. He FLASHBACKS.

FLASHBACK. INT. HOTEL BEDROOM - DAY

Debra, fully dressed, tosses $100 bill at Nakata in bed.

>   NAKATA
>   What's this?

>   DEBRA MARTINS
>   A hundred. What I usually pay.

>   NAKATA
>   Pay! I'm no gig—

>   DEBRA MARTINS
>   A good ride's all you were to me.

EXITS. Nakata rips the $100.

BACK TO PRESENT. INT. NAKATA'S SHRINE - DAY

Nakata conflicts whether Martins, having had an immoral wife like Debra, should be killed.

INT. KITCHEN. DANIEL MARTINS' HOUSE, EAST HAMPTON - DAY

Daniel Martins drinks coffee with housekeeper, ALICE, 70.

>   DANIEL
>   I'm going to finish packing, Alice.

>   ALICE
>   I hope you'll be happy, Mr Martins.
>   Miss Nakata's a lovely lady.

>   DANIEL
>   Thank you, Alice. I will be.

Exits, goes upstairs.

>   ALICE
>   (depth of feeling)
>   Oh, I hope so. Especially after *her*.

INT. NAKATA'S APARTMENT - DAY

Nakata can't decide about Martins, takes Rachel and Emma's photo to his sofa. Broods. FLASHBACKS.

FLASHBACK. INT. SOFTLY LIT BEDROOM - NIGHT

Rachel lies in bed, but days to live, propped-up by a nest of pillows. Nakata sits on the bed holding her hand.

                    RACHEL
              (voice weak)
          Tell Emma all about me, John. And
          tell her I loved her so much.

                    NAKATA
              (chokes with emotion)
          I will, Rach, I promise.

                    RACHEL
              (pleads)
          Take care of her. Never let her be
          without.

Rachel's voice cracks. She forces herself to continue.

                    RACHEL (CONT'D)
          Meg, too. She's been a tower of
          strength these last months. And
          Emma loves her so much.

Nakata nods, too choked to speak. Rachel extends her arms
to be held. He clasps her gently, yet firmly, secure.

INT. NAKATA'S APARTMENT - DAY

Nakata comes out of his Flashback, wipes tears, phones out
on his personal landline, gets Meg's answer-service.

                    MEG'S VOICE
          You've reached Meg. Please leave
          a message.

                    NAKATA
          Meg. John. I may be passing near
          you later today. If so, I'll call
          by to see you and Emma. But don't
          spoil it for her by telling her,
          in case my plans change.

INT. MEG'S HOUSE - DAY

Sitting room. Meg is talking on phone to Daniel.

                    DANIEL (O.S)
          Don't worry. I love you too much to
          drive fast and take risks.

                    MEG
          I love you, too. Can't wait to hold
          you.

                    DANIEL (O.S)
          Nor me, you.

INT. OUTER HALLWAY, WARNER'S LUXURY APARTMENT - DAY

Lisa rings doorbell. Waits. Suspects she's being studied through security-viewer.

>   LISA
>   I'd like to speak to Mrs Susan
>   Warner, if possible. Personal.

Susan, now dressed, no make-up, opens door, wary.

>   SUSAN
>   I'm Susan Warner.

>   LISA
>   Lisa. Lisa Perano.

Susan waits for Lisa to explain what she's here for.

>   LISA (CONT'D)
>   I'm hoping you can help me locate
>   someone? In his early-thirties?
>   Part Japanese?

Susan hesitates, moves aside.

>   SUSAN
>   You'd best come in.

INT. DANIEL'S BEDROOM - DAY

Daniel is still on phone to Meg. A suitcase is packed.

>   MEG (O.S.)
>   When are you starting off?

>   DANIEL
>   Right away.

>   MEG (O.S.)
>   Promise again you'll take care.

>   DANIEL
>   Sure I will. I've all to live for
>   now.

Ends call, gives last look around, exits with suitcase.

INT. SITTING ROOM, WARNER'S LUXURY APARTMENT - DAY

Susan and Lisa enter the room.

Don Giovanni is on pause on TV screen, at Scene 2, with Giovanni holding Zerlina, in wedding dress, in his arms.

Susan indicates the screen.

                    SUSAN
          The man you're asking about. It's
          how we met. At the Opera House.

Indicates DVD cover of *Don Giovanni* to Lisa.

                    SUSAN (CONT'D)
          Don Giovanni. He sat next to me.

Invites Lisa to sit, does so herself, starts to tell Lisa about Nakata.

                    SUSAN (CONT'D)
          What can I tell you about him. He
          was charming ...

LATER

Susan concludes telling Lisa about Nakata.

                    SUSAN
          The strange thing - just for an
          hour there in his room - he made
          me feel like I meant something
          to him.

Adds, with a please-don't-judge-me plea.

                    SUSAN (CONT'D)
          Like he was taking me up into
          the heavens. It was a whole new
          sensation I'd never experienced
          before.
                    (sarcastic)
          Certainly not with Bob! Ten years
          married to him, and he'd still no
          idea how to make a woman feel loved.

Confides to Lisa.

                    SUSAN (CONT'D)
          But during my hour alone with ...
                    (pauses, wistful)
          ... I'm sure I saw the man he was,
          not the man he's become.

                    LISA
          He's not even that anymore.

                    SUSAN
                    (realistic now)
          No, I realize that now.

Lisa waits for Susan to explain.

                    SUSAN (CONT'D)
          He killed Bob. I saw him leave.

                    LISA
          Excluding a forger and a mugger,
          he's now killed nine men.

                    SUSAN
                (horrified)
          Nine!

                    LISA
          I know why the mugger, but not the
          others. Nor what's driving him on.

                    SUSAN
          Have you told the police?

                    LISA
          If you can't help me - I will.

The pause on *Don Giovanni* ends. Screen goes black.

                    SUSAN
          I know where he lives.

INT. NAKATA'S APARTMENT - DAY

Nakata kneels at his shrine. Slits Daniel Martins' face.

          NAKATA   TRANSLATION
     Kore hajixyuuoo jigokuwo   This is the tenth soul for
     saibankanno no tamashiiha   Juo, the ten Judges of Hell
     desu.   to rule on.

Shuts Ledger, promises Rachel.

                    NAKATA
          After this, Rach, there will be
          no more. I will have redeemed
          myself and my life can again be
          with Emma.

Bows to shrine. Stands. Enters bedroom.

INT. LISA'S CAR - DAY

Lisa speeds to Nakata's apartment.

INT. NAKATA'S APARTMENT - DAY

Wearing black - leather jacket, trousers, polo-neck sweater
- Nakata exits his bedroom, pockets tanto. EXITS apartment.

INT. LISA'S CAR - DAY

Lisa nears Nakata's apartment.

EXT. NAKATA'S APARTMENTS HOUSE - DAY

Nakata's gets into his SUV, starts down road. Lisa's car comes down the road from behind it, brakes hard outside.

INT. NAKATA'S SUV - DAY

In rear mirror, Nakata sees Lisa exit her car, pat pocket, a give-away she has a gun, run into his building. Realizes someone is on to him. Checks pistol in compartment, speeds off.

EXT. OUTER HALLWAY, NAKATA'S APARTMENT - DAY

Lisa checks loaded revolver, rings doorbell. No answer. Rings bell again. No answer. Pulls revolver, kicks door in. Enters.

INT. NAKATA'S APARTMENT - DAY

Lisa closes door behind her, sees shrine, takes in:

-- Kneeling stool, tapers, closed black leather Ledger.
-- Framed photo, with black ribbon, of Rachel and Emma.
-- Portrait of robed Nakata and Rachel above shrine.

Sees Fontana painting on wall. In her ear, hears Gina ask:

                    GINA (V/O)
      Why would a Polish forger slit
      his throat with a samurai tanto?

Lisa broods over it, turns away, checks rest of apartment, finds nothing of interest, returns to shrine.

She picks up Rachel and Emma's photo, studies their faces, fingers black ribbon, replaces photo on table.

Picks up Ledger, flicks through it, realizes what it is.

Reaches Daniel Martins' page, sees face is slit. So is the one after him: Luke Van Allen's, alongside Abby's photo.

Next page is Jake Ross's, face slit, with Mia Ross's photo. Next is Tony Falco, face slit. She dwells a moment on Anna's pretty face, then flicks on:

-- Edward Cooper, face slit, and Olivia Cooper.
-- Carl Torres, face slit, and Ava Torres.
-- David Perry, face slit, and Grace Perry.

Lisa turns to next page: Tracie with Saul Braunstein. His
face is sliced with many cuts, and crossed with lines.

Turns to Warner's page, face slit, and Susan Warner.
Turns to James Hagen's page, face slit, and Julia Hagan.
Turns to next page. BLANK. So are pages from therein.

Re-flicks BACK from Hagan. Realizes pages are in the reverse
order that the victims, other than Braunstein, were killed.

Re-reaches Daniel Martins' page, and sees faces of previous
"clients" to the start of the Ledger have NOT been slit.

Lisa looks again at Daniel Martins, realises he's Nakata's
next victim ... IF HE'S NOT ALREADY BEEN KILLED

INT. NAKATA'S SUV - DAY

Nakata drives through N.Y. heading for Williamsburg Bridge.

INT. NAKATA'S APARTMENT - DAY

Lisa puts Ledger, showing Daniel Martins' page, aside.

Sees DVD cover of VENGEANCE IS MINE on coffee table and two
rolled-up illustrations under sofa cushions. Spreads them on
coffee table, sees they are of:

-- Noguchi's Death (Lynched Figure).
-- Dali's Crucifixion (Corpus Hypecubus).

Deliberates over them, and cover of VENGEANCE IS MINE.

Looks again at Martins' page.
Is he still alive? Or is he dead?

Phones only number, a landline, on Martins' page.

EXT. DANIEL MARTINS' HOUSE - DAY

It has a Realtor's FOR SALE board at end of the drive.
Daniel briefly hugs Alice before getting into his car.

                    DANIEL
          I won't say goodbye, Alice.

Phone inside house rings. Alice turns to answer it.

                    DANIEL (CONT'D)
          Leave it, it can't be urgent. I'll
          call you when I get to Meg's. And
          I'll drive over every so often to
          make sure you're okay.

                              ALICE
                        (teary)
                  Thank you, Mr. Martins. And for my
                  pension. It's really generous of you.

                              DANIEL
                  You're worth every cent of it, Alice,
                  putting up with me as you've done.

                              ALICE
                  It was my pleasure, Mr. Martins.

Martins' phone inside house stops ringing.

INT. NAKATA'S APARTMENT - DAY

Lisa gets Daniel Martins' answerphone.

                              DANIEL'S VOICE
                  This is Daniel Martins. Sorry I'm
                  not able to take your call -

She cuts call, phones Gina, gets her answer-message.

                              GINA (V.O.)
                  Gina Cambi, newsroom. I'm not at my
                  desk at the moment. Leave a message.

                              LISA
                  Gina it's Lisa. Call me, it's urgent.

EXITS with Nakata's Ledger.

Nakata's LANDLINE rings. Answerphone switches on.

                              NAKATA'S VOICE
                  Leave your number, I'll phone back.

                              MEG (O.S.)
                  John, I got your message. Hope you
                  haven't changed your plans, we'd
                  love to see you. I've also just
                  seen the huge transfer you made
                  to my account. What's that about?

EXT. DANIEL MARTINS' HOUSE - DAY

Daniel's car moves off, window lowered.

                              DANIEL
                  Take good care of yourself, Alice.

                              ALICE
                  You, too, Mr. Martins.

Alice waves Daniel out of sight.

                    ALICE (CONT'D)
And be happy! God knows you deserve it after *her*.

Heads back for the house.

INT. LISA'S CAR - DAY

Lisa gets into her car. Her cell rings. Sees it's Gina. Replies before Gina speaks.

                    LISA
Gina. Have there been any suicides reported in East Hampton?

                    GINA (O.S.)
Not that we've heard of. Why?

                    LISA
I think a Daniel Martins could be next. I tried calling him but he's on answerphone. His number is -

                    GINA (O.S)
Hold on ... Shoot.

                    LISA
631 429 8766. Try him for me. Let me know if you get no success and we'll both keep trying until one of us gets through. This could be our chance to get the louse for what he did to Anna.

Cuts call. Drives off.

INT. GINA'S NEWSROOM - DAY

Gina dials out. She gets Martins' answerphone.

                    DANIEL'S VOICE
This is Daniel Martins. Sorry I'm not able to -

Message cuts off as Alice answers.

                    ALICE (O.S.)
This is Alice. Mr Martins' house-keeper.

                    GINA
Alice. I need to talk to Mr Martins.

                    ALICE (O.S.)
          Who is this?

                    GINA
          Gina Gambi, New York Sentinel.

                    ALICE (O.S.)
          I'm afraid Mr Martins' just left.

                    GINA
          Can you tell me where he's making
          for? And the phone number there.

                    ALICE (O.S.)
          I'd have to speak to Mr. Martins
          first. I'll call his cell-phone.

                    GINA
          I'd like that number too. And
          hurry please, Alice. It's urgent.
          I'll call back in two minutes.

INT. LISA'S CAR - DAY

Lisa picks up her ringing cell as she drives.

                    GINA (O.S.)
          Martins' still alive, but I failed
          to get hold of him. Housekeeper
          says he's on his way somewhere. I'm
          calling her back in two minutes for
          the address and his cell number.

Lisa makes an instant decision.

                    LISA
          I'll head for Martins' home. I have
          the address. Let me know where he's
          making for as soon as you get it.
                    (adds)
          And call Hampton police.

Cuts call, checks Martins' address in Ledger, speeds up.

INT. NAKATA'S SUV - DAY

Nakata drives across Williamsburg Bridge on to Long Island.
He's driving carefully, nothing must stop him from redeeming
himself with this tenth and last death.

EXT. ROMAN CATHOLIC CHURCH, GREENWICH - DAY

Lisa sees church, slams to a halt outside it. Runs in.

INT. ROMAN CATHOLIC CHURCH, GREENWICH - DAY

Lisa enters, sees O'Donnell near altar, hurries to him.

LISA
I'm in a hell of a hurry - sorry Father, I'm in a rush, but hoping you can solve something for me.

O'Donnell waits for her to continue.

LISA (CONT'D)
It looks like this Waka guy is killing off the husbands who paid him, but making their deaths look like suicides.

O'DONNELL
Then you must inform the police.

LISA
A friend's doing it right now. It's just that ...

O'DONNELL
Yes?

LISA
I got into his apartment -

Cuts across O'Donnell before he can ask how?

LISA (CONT'D)
There were two pictures. One of the Crucifixion. The other - it looked Japanese - of a man trapped inside a cage with a noose around his neck.

O'DONNELL
I know it. A Noguchi sculpture.

LISA
My first thought was that in some crazy way, the guy's seeking ... well, redemption?

O'DONNELL
But now you're not sure?

LISA
It doesn't conform. If forgiveness for his sins is what he's after, why's he adding more by committing murder?

Her cell rings, sees it's Gina.

LISA (CONT'D)
Sorry, Father, I have to take this.
(switches on cell)
Gina?

GINA (O.S)
(urgent)
Hampton police can only promise to send a car soon as one's available.

LISA
Thanks, Gina.

Cuts call, wants answers in a hurry from O'Donnell.

LISA
Can you give it me in as few words as possible, Father.

O'DONNELL
Then I suspect the answer lies in the oriental side of his psyche. There's an ancient Japanese song, coincidentally called *Redemption*, that contains these words ...
(quotes them)
What else can I do besides avenge thee?

LISA
You mean the killings are not for himself? But to avenge the wrongs done by the husbands to their wives?

O'DONNELL
That would be my conclusion, Lisa.

LISA
But why kill the husbands and not the wives? They're just as much to blame. Willing to be seduced. *Even Anna.*

O'DONNELL
Because - I again suspect - that he hates himself for what he is. His ... his chosen profession. And so blames the men who paid him, not their wives.

Despite being on edge to be off, Lisa has last question.

LISA
Still on the Japanese scenario, what will he do when he's killed them all?

                    O'DONNELL
          Either return to his old life, his
          honour satisfied. Or ...

                    LISA
          Or?

                    O'DONNELL
          He'll commit seppuku –

                    LISA
          Seppuku?

Old priest thinks Lisa doesn't know what this means.

                    O'DONNELL
          Ritual suicide. Disembowelment. Wrongly
          believing he will thus enter a land of
          pure bliss, and be reunited with lost
          loved ones.

                    LISA
          I think he's lost his wife. Maybe a
          daughter, too.

                    O'DONNELL
          Then that is what I suspect he will
          most likely do.

                    LISA
          I *have* to go, Father.

She hurries up the aisle. O'Donnell calls after her.

                    O'DONNELL
          Lisa.

Lisa semi-glances back as she goes, on edge to be off.

                    LISA
          Yes, Father?

                    O'DONNELL
          Whatever you're searching for, don't
          neglect your soul. Anna was her own
          person. You're in NO way responsible
          for her death –

                    LISA
              (dismissive)
          Sure, Father.

                    O'DONNELL
          You need to give thought to your own
          life again. As Anna would have wanted
          you to do.

                    LISA
          Received, Father. Can I go now?

                    O'DONNELL
          With my blessing, Lisa.

Watches Lisa EXIT in a hurry. Makes sign of the Cross.

                    O'DONNELL (CONT'D)
          And the blessing of Almighty God.

INT. DANIEL MARTINS' HOUSE - DAY

Alice talks to Daniel on his cell.

                    ALICE
          She said it's urgent, Mr Martins.

INT. DANIEL'S CAR - DAY

Daniel, heading West past East Hampton, answers Alice.

                    DANIEL
          Give her Meg's address and phone
          number, Alice. But not my cell.
          It can't be that urgent.

                    ALICE (O.S.)
          Very well, Mr. Martins.

Daniel ends call, continues West on Route 27.

INT. NAKATA'S SUV - DAY

Nakata exits Queens Expressway and makes for Route 495, to head East across Long Island.

INT. LISA'S CAR - DAY

Lisa speeds through N.Y. making for Williamsburg Bridge.

INT. GINA'S NEWSROOM - DAY

Gina re-calls Alice, speaks as soon as Alice picks up.

                    GINA
          Alice, it's me again. Can you give
          me the address and phone numbers?

                    ALICE (O.S.)
          Mr Martins said not his cellphone.

                    GINA
          Oh, for fuck's sake ...!

Shocked at Gina's language, Alice frostily adds:

                    ALICE
          But I can give you the address and
          number of where he's driving to.

                    GINA
          Then spill them, Alice. Sorry for
          my expletive. Blame the urgency.

INT. LISA'S CAR - DAY

Lisa crosses Williamsburg Bridge, making for Route 495.
Her cell rings. Answers it.

                    GINA (O.S.)
          I've got the address and phone of
          where he's headed, but not his cell.

                    LISA
          Give me the address.

Enters address in GPS as Gina gives it.

                    LISA (CONT'D)
               (urgent)
          I'm on my way! And keep calling
          him until you get him!

Switches off cell, speeds up.

INT. MEG'S HOUSE, FRONT HALL - DAY

Meg enters Hall from the kitchen, picks up car keys from
a phone table, hears house-keeper, MARIA, 50, singing to
herself upstairs.

                    MEG
          Maria!

Maria exits bedroom to the landing.

                    MARIA
          Si, Miss Nakata?

                    MEG
          I'm going to pick up Emma. I should
          be back in under an hour.

                    MARIA
          Very good, Miss Nakata.

Meg exits. Maria re-enters bedroom, switches on vacuum, resumes singing. Hall phone rings. Answerphone replies.

> MEG'S VOICE
> You've reached Meg. Please leave a message.

> GINA (O.S.)
> Gina Campi, New York Sentinel with a message for Daniel Martins ...
> (waits, no one picks up)
> It's urgent he calls me the instant he arrives. On number ...

INT. LISA'S CAR - DAY

Lisa exits Queens Expressway on to Route 495, heads East across Long Island.

INT. NAKATA'S SUV - DAY

Nakata heads East on Route 495, miles ahead of Lisa.

INT. DANIEL'S CAR - DAY

Daniel heads West on Route 27 from South Fork.

EXT. GAS STATION, MEG'S NEAREST TOWN - DAY

The town is a mile East of Meg's house. Meg exits station after taking on gas, checks the time, speeds away.

INT. DANIEL'S CAR - DAY

Daniel by-passes Southampton, still heads West on Route 27.

INT. NAKATA'S SUV - DAY

Nakata nears the end of Route 495, phones Meg's home.

> MEG'S VOICE
> You've reached Meg. Please leave a message.

Cuts call, tries her cell.

INT. MEG'S CAR - DAY

Meg heads for Emma's school, answers her cell.

                    MEG
          Meg Nakata.

                    NAKATA (O.S.)
          Meg. It's John.

                    MEG
          John! *Twice* in four days!

INT. NAKATA'S SUV - DAY

                    NAKATA
          I'm meeting a client who lives on
          Long Island, then coming to spend
          the day with you and Emma.

                    MEG (O.S.)
          Oh, John, Emma will be so thrilled.
          John ...? About the money you paid
          into my account ...?

                    NAKATA
          For the moment, let's say I'm
          liquidating my assets, hoping to -

Sees his exit off Route 495 on to Route 24 approaching.

                    NAKATA (CONT'D)
          Meg, I'm approaching my off-slip -

                    MEG (O.S.)
          John! Before you go, I've met some -

                    NAKATA
          You can tell me when I see you.

Cuts call, exits on to Route 24 East, for Daniel's home in South Fork.

INT. DANIEL'S CAR - DAY

Daniel exits Route 27 on to Route 24 West, for Emma's home in North Fork.

INT. NAKATA'S SUV - DAY

Nakata recognises Daniel drive past in opposite direction. Nakata U-turns, follows Daniel from a safe distance.

INT. DANIEL'S CAR - DAY

Daniel phones Meg's home.

                    MEG'S VOICE
          You've reached Meg. Please leave a
          message.

Daniel cuts the call, tries Meg's cell.

INT. MEG'S CAR - DAY

Meg nears Emma's school, answers her cell.

                    DANIEL (O.S.)
          Meg, I should be with you in -

                    MEG
          John's just called.

INT. DANIEL'S CAR - DAY

Meg expands to Daniel.

                    MEG (CONT'D O.S.)
          He's here on Long Island to see a
          client, then calling to see Emma.

Daniel sees Nakata's black SUV in his rear mirror.

                    DANIEL
          So, I'm finally going to meet him.

Looks away from mirror.

                    MEG (O.S)
          I'm sure you'll get along grand.

INT. MEG'S CAR - DAY

Meg sees Emma in new uniform waiting outside new school.

                    MEG
          I have to go, Dan, Emma's waiting.

                    DANIEL (O.S.)
          Meg, there may be a message for me
          on your answerphone -

                    MEG
          I love you.
              (cuts call)

Meg stops for Emma to get into the car, hugs her.

                    MEG (CONT'D)
          Sorry I'm late.

                         EMMA
               That's okay.

                         MEG
               Before you tell me about your new
               school, I've some exciting news.

INT. NAKATA'S SUV - DAY

Nakata follows Daniel as they re-pass Route 495 exit, and
continue heading East along Route 24 for North Fork.

INT. DANIEL'S CAR - DAY

Daniel re-checks black SUV in his mirror, is puzzled by it.
It almost seems to be tailing him.

INT. LISA'S CAR - DAY

Lisa's GPS tells her to take next exit off Route 495. Sees
it ahead. Cell rings. Picks it up.

                         GINA (O.S.)
                    (rushes her words)
               I called that number. All I got was
               an answerphone. I left a message -

                         LISA
               It's okay. I'm almost there. Got to
               go, I'm nearing my exit road.

                         GINA (O.S.)
               Lisa! Take care!

Lisa exits onto Route 24 and heads for North Fork, a mile or
so behind Nakata and Daniel.

EXT. DANIEL MARTINS' HOUSE - DAY

A Hampton Police patrol car comes up to house. Alice hurries
out of house to it, all anxious to get the police's help.

POLICE DRIVER questions Alice through his open window. She
blurts to him where Daniel is heading for.

                         POLICE DRIVER
               North Fork. That's not within our
               jurisdiction. I'll call Greenport
               Police when I get back to station.

                         ALICE
               But -

                                POLICE DRIVER
                        Don't worry, ma'am. They'll get
                        someone on to it.
                                (drives off)

INT. DANIEL'S CAR - DAY

Daniel exits Route 24 onto two-lane Route 48. On his left
is a rocky shore-line, overlooking Long Island Sound.

Looks in his mirror. Black SUV is still behind him. Its
driver is a dark silhouette.

INT. MEG'S CAR - DAY

Meg stops outside store. Emma can't contain her excitement.

                                EMMA
                        What is it, Mummy? Is Daddy coming
                        to live with us?

Unsure how to explain all that's happening, Meg compromises.

                                MEG
                        Yes; and sooner than you think. He
                        may even be waiting for us at home.

                                EMMA
                        Yippee!

Meg hugs Emma again, enters store. Emma waits, all agog.

INT. DANIEL'S CAR - DAY

Daniel is now on two-lane Route 48. Turns left onto track
to Meg's house, built alone overlooking Long Island Sound.

INT. NAKATA'S SUV - DAY

Nakata's never seen Meg's new house. Stops. Watches Daniel
drive around it from sight. Considers his next move.

INT. MEG'S CAR - DAY

Meg exits store with bag of groceries, gets into car, heads
West out of town for home. Emma is still excited.

EXT. BACK OF MEG'S HOUSE - DAY

Daniel exits his car, enters house.

INT. MEG'S HOUSE - DAY

Daniel enters kitchen. Maria's drinking coffee.

MARIA
Miss Nakata not be long, Mr Martins. She picking Emma up from school.

DANIEL
I'll go for a stroll on the headland, Maria. Clear my head after driving.

MARIA
I tell Miss Nakata, Mr Martins.

Daniel exits.

INT. LISA'S CAR - DAY

Lisa sees a black SUV parked by side of road ahead of her.

Obeys an instinct, stops, sees SUV has NY license, but can see only top of driver's head above seat headrest.

Sees Meg's house in near distance, switches off her GPS.

INT. NAKATA'S SUV - DAY

Nakata sees Daniel come from behind the house and head in his direction. Nakata takes in the lay of the headland.

Sees copse overlooking an outcrop of rock near cliff-edge. He drives across headland to copse, enters it.

Through trees, he sees Daniel approaching a way off, but coming nearer.

INT. MEG'S CAR - DAY

Meg gets home, drives to back of house. Emma sees Daniel's car, tumbles out of Meg's car, runs into the kitchen.

Meg, with her groceries bag, follows Emma into house.

INT. MEG'S HOUSE - DAY

Meg enters kitchen. Maria's consoling Emma who runs to Meg. Meg puts her groceries down, looks at Maria for explanation.

MARIA
Mr. Martins gone for walk, Miss Nakata.

                    MEG
               (to Emma)
          Shall we go after him?

                    EMMA
          Yes! Yes!

                    MARIA
          I think you have phone message,
          Miss Nakata.

Meg and Emma enter Front Hall. Meg plays Gina's message.

                    GINA'S VOICE
          Gina Campi, New York Sentinel with
          a message for Daniel Martins. It's
          urgent he calls me the instant he
          arrives. On number -

Meg cuts message, dampens her concern not to upset Emma.

                    MEG
          I wonder what that's all about?

Takes Emma's hand. They EXIT by front door

EXT. FRONT OF MEG'S HOUSE - DAY

Meg sees Daniel walking in the distance across headland.

                    MEG
          Race you. But not too fast. We
          don't want your baby brother
          born too soon.

They hurry after Daniel.

INT. NAKATA'S SUV - DAY

From the copse, Nakata sees Daniel go behind the outcrop.
Pockets his pistol with his tanto, exits his SUV.

EXT. COPSE - DAY

Nakata waits for Daniel to reappear from around outcrop.

INT. LISA'S CAR - DAY

Lisa edges her car to where SUV had previously stopped on
road. Sees it hiding in copse, and a man standing by it.

Daniel comes into Lisa's view from behind the outcrop.

Lisa sees man exit copse and head across headland to meet Daniel. She guesses who both men are, pulls her revolver.

Lisa now sees Meg and Emma in the distance, running after Daniel. Lisa heads her car for copse.

EXT. HEADLAND, EAST OF OUTCROP - DAY

Meg calls to the still distant Daniel.

                     MEG
      Daniel! Daniel!

He doesn't hear her, goes from her sight around outcrop. Emma pulls her hand free from Meg's, races ahead of her.

EXT. HEADLAND, WEST OF OUTCROP - DAY

Nakata pulls pistol, walks toward Daniel who recognizes him from the past.

Daniel backs away, toward cliff. The sun is sinking low on the horizon. It has a red Japanese look about it.

INT. LISA'S CAR - DAY

Lisa enters copse, sees Nakata, pistol drawn, closing on Daniel. Fires warning shot from her window, exits car.

EXT. HEADLAND, EAST OF OUTCROP - DAY

Meg hears shot, can't see Daniel or Nakata, but whatever is happening, Emma is running toward it. Meg panics, runs.

                     MEG
      Emma! Emma!

Emma runs around outcrop from Meg's sight.

EXT. HEADLAND, WEST OF OUTCROP - DAY

Nakata hears shot, sees Lisa run out of the copse, revolver drawn. Recognizes her from an hour ago.

FLASHCUT: Lisa runs from her car into his apartment building.

Nakata realizes Lisa's after him, but advances on Daniel who backs to CLIFF EDGE.

Lisa trains her revolver on Nakata as she runs, but he's now too close to Daniel to risk a shot.

Emma runs around outcrop, sees Nakata, Daniel and Lisa.

                    EMMA
               (exclaims)
          Daddy!

Nakata spins around, sees Emma, freezes.

EXT. HEADLAND, EAST OF OUTCROP - DAY

Still running after Emma, Meg falls to her knees, holding her womb.

EXT. HEADLAND, WEST OF OUTCROP - DAY

Rocks crumble under Daniel's feet. Slides over the edge but grips on, dangling over sheer drop to sea below.

Emma is rendered speechless, numb with fear for him.

EXT. HEADLAND, EAST OF OUTCROP - DAY

Meg struggles to rise, but can't.

EXT. HEADLAND, WEST OF OUTCROP - DAY

Emma runs past Nakata, looks helplessly down at Daniel.

                    EMMA
               (sobs)
          Daddy! Daddy!

Daniel looks up imploringly at Nakata. Nakata hesitates. Daniel's grip starts to slip. Emma whimpers.

Nakata drops pistol, pulls Daniel to safety. Emma grips Daniel's legs tight.

                    EMMA (O.S.)
          Daddy! Daddy!

Daniel picks up Emma. Sees Lisa, revolver pointed only at Nakata. Daniel hotfoots it from whatever's happening here.

Over Daniel's shoulder, Emma looks at Nakata. He reaches out his arms to her. Emma turns away.

Nakata drops to his knees in despair on cliff edge. Daniel hurries with Emma around the outcrop from sight.

Lisa reaches Nakata, revolver trained on him. He can't get to his pistol. Red sun's dipping down on the sea's horizon.

EXT. HEADLAND, EAST OF OUTCROP - DAY

Daniel rounds outcrop, sees Meg on her knees. Puts Emma down, runs to Meg and gently helps her to her feet. His worry about her is now by far uppermost in his mind.

DANIEL
Are you alright?

MEG
Fine. Just want to get home and lie down. What was that gunshot?

Daniel's more concerned about Meg, anxious to get her away from what's happening beyond outcrop. Replies dismissive.

DANIEL
Just someone taking a pot-shot at a gull. Missed by a mile.

Puts a supporting arm around Meg. Emma takes his free hand. They head for home.

EXT. HEADLAND, WEST OF OUTCROP - DAY

Lisa points her revolver at Nakata. He produces his tanto.

LISA
If you're hoping for some hari-kari redemption - think again.

Shoots him in the stomach. Tanto drops from his hand. He falls back off the cliff.

EXT. HEADLAND, EAST OF OUTCROP - DAY

Daniel and Meg hear second gunshot. He cuts in first.

DANIEL
Nothing to do with us. Couldn't hit an elephant at two paces.

He, Meg, Emma, continue for home, as fast as Daniel dares.

EXT. HEADLAND, WEST OF OUTCROP - DAY

Lisa ambles to cliff-edge. Dispassionately watches Nakata, arms outstretched crucifixion-like, blood seeping from him, start to float out to sea on a red beam emanating from the sinking sun.

She tosses pistol into the sea, has no further use for it. Kicks tanto after it. Heads back for her car.

EXT. LONG ISLAND SOUND - DAY

Floating out to sea, Nakata looks at sun now mostly below horizon. Gets VISION of Rachel extending her arms to him.

Sun dips from Nakata's sight, extinguishing its red beam and his vision of Rachel. Water around him is now grey.

Suddenly it's BLACKNESS.

INT. LISA'S CAR - SAME TIME

Lisa heads car up the copse lane. Calls Gina, speaks first.

              LISA
    Objective eliminated, Gina. Tell
    you tomorrow. Your place. And
    thanks for your help. I couldn't
    have done it without you.

Cuts call. Exits on to two-lane Route 48, heads for home.

A 100-yards ahead on her right, a male back-packer wearing army-camouflage combats emerges from a lane, pauses by side of the road to allow her to pass him.

He's young, good-looking, rugged with a dark stubble. Lisa stops, lowers passenger side window. He looks in.

              LISA
    Where're you headed?

            BACKPACKER
    New York.

              LISA
    You're in luck. Get in.

He gets in. Lisa resumes driving. She sees his Afghanistan campaign ribbon, mostly red, white, black, on his shirt.

              LISA
    Ghan? Where were you based?

            BACKPACKER
    Bagram.

              LISA
    Same here.

            BACKPACKER
    Yeah. Used to see you around the
    camp. Thought you were kinda cute.
        (grins)
    Even in combats.

                    LISA
          And out of them?

                    BACKPACKER
          Hundred and ten per cent right.

EXT. LISA'S CAR - SAME TIME

Car heads for New York. Lisa hums Cagney and Lacey theme
tune O.S. Breaks it.

                    LISA (O.S.)
          Got a place for the night?

                    BACKPACKER (O.S.)
          Bench. Central Park.

                    LISA (O.S.)
          I know somewhere you can stay.

                    BACKPACKER (O.S.)
          Does it have a bed?

Lisa replies to herself in a low murmur.

                    LISA (O.S.)
          You bet it does.

Re-hums Cagney and Lacey theme tune as car gets smaller
into the distance.

                                                  FADE OUT

          THE END

Richard Rees

Richard Rees is originally from Wrexham, North Wales, where he had an accountancy practice, but became a writer after the deaths of his young wife, Richenda, then his only daughter, Elisabeth, from ovarian cancer. He now lives a quiet life in the seaside town of Llandudno, at the foot of the Snowdonia National Park, doesn't drink or smoke, and so sounds a bit of a bore, but is gregarious, keeps fit, swims, drives fast and doesn't play golf.

For more information on Richard's books, including where to purchase them, or to contact Richard, go to

www.richardhrees.com

Novels by Richard Rees

The Illuminati Conspiracy

The Reikel Conspiracy

Twice Upon A Thanksgiving

Dear Abigail

Somebody Wants to Kill Me

Screenplays by Richard Rees

Diabolus in Musica: A story of Niccolo Paganini

Printed in Great Britain
by Amazon